MW01063284

BIBLE
VITALS

FACTS,
FIGURES, FAITH,
AND FUN

Tracy M. Sumner

BARBOUR
PUBLISHING

Published by Barbour Publishing, Inc., P.O. Box 719, Uhrichsville, Ohio 44683, www.barbourbooks.com

Our mission is to publish and distribute inspirational products offering exceptional value and biblical encouragement to the masses.

Member of the
Evangelical Christian
Publishers Association

Printed in the United States of America.

CONTENTS

INTRODUCTION

If someone were to ask what you believed was the best thing about reading the Bible, how would you answer? Would you say the Bible is filled with amazing history? That it tells fascinating stories about great men and women of God? Or would you answer that it instructs through example how you can be a success and how you can avoid failure in your walk with God?

None of those answers would be wrong, but the Bible isn't just a book filled with stories about people who lived a long time ago in a faraway land; it's the 66-book story of how God interacted with those people and how they interacted with Him. It's the God-inspired account of how God created the heavens, the earth, and humankind. . .and how He has worked and is working to bring about the redemption of creation and of those who place their trust in Him. And it's God's own communication with you!

Knowing all this, is it any wonder that God has commanded and encouraged His people to read, study, and meditate on the Bible?

There are many ways you can study the Bible for yourself. You can read it cover to cover, study different topics, or concentrate on one book at a time. Another great way to study the Bible is to focus on specific people and events. . .and on God's part in their lives and the events that took place.

That's what the little book you're holding in your hands is for!

This book is essentially a collection of lists—lists about the Bible itself, about God Himself, and about the people, places, and events you can find in the pages of the Good Book. Our hope is that you, the reader, can use these lists to help make your study of the Bible easier, more enjoyable, and more beneficial to your growth in Jesus Christ!

SIXTY-SIX BOOKS IN ONE: THE BIBLE AND HOW WE GOT IT

The word *Bible* comes from a Latin word meaning "book." And even though we take the Bible as a single Book containing the promises, commands, and wisdom of God, it is actually a collection of 66 different writings.

Here is a list of those books, first alphabetically, then as they appear in the Bible:

ALPHABETICALLY

1. 1 Chronicles
2. 1 Corinthians
3. 1 John
4. 1 Kings
5. 1 Peter
6. 1 Samuel
7. 1 Thessalonians
8. 1 Timothy
9. 2 Chronicles
10. 2 Corinthians
11. 2 John
12. 2 Kings
13. 2 Peter
14. 2 Samuel
15. 2 Thessalonians
16. 2 Timothy
17. 3 John
18. Acts
19. Amos
20. Colossians
21. Daniel
22. Deuteronomy
23. Ecclesiastes
24. Ephesians
25. Esther
26. Exodus
27. Ezekiel
28. Ezra
29. Galatians
30. Genesis
31. Habakkuk
32. Haggai

33.	Hebrews	51.	Micah
34.	Hosea	52.	Nahum
35.	Isaiah	53.	Nehemiah
36.	James	54.	Numbers
37.	Jeremiah	55.	Obadiah
38.	Job	56.	Philemon
39.	Joel	57.	Philippians
40.	John	58.	Proverbs
41.	Jonah	59.	Psalms
42.	Joshua	60.	Revelation
43.	Jude	61.	Romans
44.	Judges	62.	Ruth
45.	Lamentations	63.	Song of Solomon
46.	Leviticus		
47.	Luke	64.	Titus
48.	Malachi	65.	Zechariah
49.	Mark	66.	Zephaniah
50.	Matthew		

AS THEY APPEAR IN THE BIBLE

Old Testament

1.	Genesis	10.	2 Samuel
2.	Exodus	11.	1 Kings
3.	Leviticus	12.	2 Kings
4.	Numbers	13.	1 Chronicles
5.	Deuteronomy	14.	2 Chronicles
6.	Joshua	15.	Ezra
7.	Judges	16.	Nehemiah
8.	Ruth	17.	Esther
9.	1 Samuel	18.	Job
		19.	Psalms

20. Proverbs
21. Ecclesiastes
22. Song of Solomon
23. Isaiah
24. Jeremiah
25. Lamentations
26. Ezekiel
27. Daniel
28. Hosea
29. Joel
30. Amos
31. Obadiah
32. Jonah
33. Micah
34. Nahum
35. Habakkuk
36. Zephaniah
37. Haggai
38. Zechariah
39. Malachi

New Testament

1. Matthew
2. Mark
3. Luke
4. John
5. Acts
6. Romans
7. 1 Corinthians
8. 2 Corinthians
9. Galatians
10. Ephesians
11. Philippians
12. Colossians
13. 1 Thessalonians
14. 2 Thessalonians
15. 1 Timothy
16. 2 Timothy
17. Titus
18. Philemon
19. Hebrews
20. James
21. 1 Peter
22. 2 Peter
23. 1 John
24. 2 John
25. 3 John
26. Jude
27. Revelation

TYPES OF BOOKS IN THE BIBLE

The Old Testament and New Testament each contain five different types of writings. The Old Testament includes books of the law, history, wisdom/poetry, the major prophets, and the minor prophets. The New Testament contains the gospels, history of the early church, the Pauline epistles, the general epistles, and apocalyptic. Here is how they break down:

OLD TESTAMENT
* Law (5): Genesis, Exodus, Leviticus, Numbers, Deuteronomy
* History (12): Joshua, Judges, Ruth, 1 Samuel, 2 Samuel, 1 Kings, 2 Kings, 1 Chronicles, 2 Chronicles, Ezra, Nehemiah, Esther
* Wisdom/Poetry (5): Job, Psalms, Proverbs, Ecclesiastes, Song of Songs
* Major Prophets (5): Isaiah, Jeremiah, Lamentations, Ezekiel, Daniel
* Minor Prophets (12): Hosea, Joel, Amos, Obadiah, Jonah, Micah, Nahum, Habakkuk, Zephaniah, Haggai, Zechariah, Malachi

NEW TESTAMENT
* Gospels (4): Matthew, Mark, Luke, John
* History of the Early Church (1): Acts of the Apostles
* Pauline Epistles (13): Romans, 1 Corinthians, 2 Corinthians, Galatians, Ephesians, Philippians,

Colossians, 1 Thessalonians, 2 Thessalonians, 1 Timothy, 2 Timothy, Titus, Philemon
* General Epistles (8): Hebrews, James, 1 Peter, 2 Peter, 1 John, 2 John, 3 John, Jude
* Apocalyptic (1): Revelation

APOCRYPHA INCLUDED IN THE KING JAMES VERSION

The word *Apocrypha* means "hidden" or "secret." The books that make up the Apocrypha contain much wisdom and historical content, and they were included in the early versions of the Bible. During the time of the Protestant Reformation, however, they were omitted from the Bible for various reasons. These books are:

* 1 Esdras
* 2 Esdras
* Tobit
* Judith
* Additions to Esther
* Wisdom of Solomon
* Ecclesiasticus (Sirach)
* Baruch
* Epistle of Jeremiah
* Son of the Three Holy Children
* Story of Susanna
* Bel and the Dragon
* Prayer of Manassheh
* 1 Maccabees
* 2 Maccabees

THE BIBLE'S WRITERS

- **Genesis, Exodus, Leviticus, Deuteronomy, Numbers**—Not stated in the text, but traditionally attributed to Moses

- **Joshua**—Traditionally, Joshua himself, except for the final five verses (24:29–33), which describe Joshua's death and legacy

- **Judges**—Not certain, but thought to be Samuel

- **Ruth**—Not certain, but thought by some to be Samuel

- **1 Samuel**—Not stated. Samuel himself was likely involved, though some of the history of 1 Samuel occurs after the prophet's death

- **2 Samuel**—Unknown, but not Samuel, since the events of the book take place after his death. Some suggest Abiathar the priest (see 15:35).

- **1 Kings**—Unknown, but one early tradition claimed Jeremiah wrote 1 and 2 Kings

- **2 Kings**—See 1 Kings

- **1 Chronicles**—Traditionally the priest Ezra

- **2 Chronicles**—See 1 Chronicles

- **Ezra**—Traditionally the priest Ezra himself (see 7:11)

- **Nehemiah**—This book is called "the words of Nehemiah" (1:1), though Jewish tradition holds that those words were put on paper by Ezra

- **Esther**—Not known for certain; possibly Ezra, Nehemiah, or Mordecai

- **Job**—Not certain, though some scholars believe Moses or Solomon wrote it

- **Psalms**—Several authors, with nearly half attributed to King David. Other names noted include Solomon, Moses, Asaph, Ethan, and the sons of Korah. Many psalms don't mention an author.

- **Proverbs**—King Solomon wrote the first twenty-nine chapters, and Agur and Lemuel wrote chapters 30 and 31.

- **Ecclesiastes**—Not stated, but probably Solomon. The author is identified as "the son of David" (1:1) and "king over Israel in Jerusalem" (1:12), and says he had "more wisdom than all they that have been before me" (1:16).

- **Song of Solomon** (or Song of Songs)—Solomon (1:1), though some wonder if the song "of Solomon" is like the psalms "of David"—which could mean they're *by, for,* or *about* him.

- **Isaiah**—The prophet Isaiah, the son of Amoz (1:1).

- **Jeremiah**—The prophet Jeremiah (1:1), with the assistance of Baruch, a scribe (36:4).

- **Lamentations**—Traditionally attributed to the prophet Jeremiah.

- **Ezekiel**—Ezekiel, a priest (1:1–3).

- **Daniel**—Likely Daniel, though some question this. Chapters 7–12 are written in the first person ("I Daniel," 7:15), though the first six chapters are in the third person ("Then Daniel answered," 2:14).

- **Hosea**—Probably Hosea himself, though the text is in both first and third person.

- **Joel**—Joel, son of Pethuel (1:1). Little else is known about him.

- **Amos**—Amos, a shepherd from Tekoa, near Bethlehem (1:1).

- **Obadiah**—Obadiah (1:1), perhaps a person by that name, or maybe an unnamed prophet for whom "Obadiah" (meaning "servant of God") is a title.

- **Jonah**—Unclear; the story is Jonah's, but written in the third person.

- **Micah**—"The word of the LORD that came to Micah the Morasthite" (1:1). Micah either wrote the prophecies or dictated them to another.

- **Nahum**—"The book of the vision of Nahum the Elkoshite" (1:1). Nahum either wrote the prophecies or dictated them to another.

- **Habakkuk**—Habakkuk (1:1); nothing is known of his background.

- **Zephaniah**—Zephaniah (1:1).

- **Haggai**—Haggai (1:1).

- **Zechariah**—Zechariah, son of Berechiah (1:1); some believe a second, unnamed writer contributed chapters 9–14.

- **Malachi**—Malachi (1:1), meaning "my messenger." No other details are given.

- **Matthew**—Traditionally Matthew, a tax collector (9:9). Matthew is also known as "Levi" (Mark 2:14).

- **Mark**—Traditionally John Mark, missionary companion of Paul and Barnabas (Acts 12:25) and associate of the apostle Peter (1 Peter 5:13).

- **Luke**—Traditionally Luke, a Gentile physician (Colossians 4:14) and missionary companion of the apostle Paul (2 Timothy 4:11).

- **John**—Traditionally John, the "disciple whom Jesus loved" (John 21:7), brother of James and son of Zebedee (Matthew 4:21).

- **Acts**—Traditionally Luke, the Gentile physician (Colossians 4:14) and missionary companion of the apostle Paul (2 Timothy 4:11), author of the Gospel of Luke.

- **Romans**—The apostle Paul (1:1), with the secretarial assistance of Tertius (16:22).

- **1 Corinthians**—The apostle Paul, with the assistance of Sosthenes (1:1).

- **2 Corinthians**—The apostle Paul, with Timothy's assistance (1:1).

- **Galatians**—The apostle Paul (1:1).

- **Ephesians**—The apostle Paul (1:1).

- **Philippians**—The apostle Paul, along with Timothy (1:1).

- **Colossians**—The apostle Paul, along with Timothy (1:1).

- **1 and 2 Thessalonians**—The apostle Paul, along with Silvanus (Silas) and Timothy (1:1).

- **1 and 2 Timothy**—The apostle Paul (1:1).

- **Titus**—The apostle Paul (1:1).

- **Philemon**—The apostle Paul, along with Timothy (1:1).

- **Hebrews**—Not known for certain. Some suggest the apostle Paul, but differences in style and tone cast doubt on his authorship. Luke, Barnabas, Phillip, Silas, and Apollos have also been suggested. It has even been suggested that Priscilla, the wife of Aquila (Priscilla and Aquila were a married couple best known for ministering to the first-century church in Corinth and Ephesus) wrote Hebrews. If that were true, Priscilla would be the only female author of a New Testament book.

- **James**—James (1:1), probably a brother of Jesus (see Matthew 13:55, Mark 6:3).

- **1 Peter**—The apostle Peter (1:1), with the assistance of Silvanus (5:12).

- **2 Peter**—The apostle Peter (1:1).

- **1 John**—According to church tradition, the apostle John.

- **2 and 3 John**—The apostle John, according to church tradition. Author is identified only as "the elder" (2 John 1; 3 John 1).

- **Jude**—Jude (1:1), possibly Jesus' half brother (see Matthew 13:55, Mark 6:3).

- **Revelation**—John (1:1), probably the apostle John, one of the Twelve.

35 IMPORTANT DATES (AND FACTS) IN BIBLE WRITING, TRANSLATION, AND PUBLISHING

* **1400 BC**—The Ten Commandments delivered to Moses

* **500–400 BC**—Completion of Hebrew manuscripts that would become the 39 Old Testament books

* **Third and Second Centuries BC**—Completion of the Septuagint, a translation of all 39 books of the Old Testament canon and the 14 books of the Apocrypha into Greek

* **1st Century AD**—Completion of all original manuscripts that make up the 27 New Testament books

* **315**—Athenasius, Bishop of Alexandria, identifies the 27 books of the New Testament

* **362**—Council of Laodicea adopts canon of Old and New Testaments and the Apocrypha

* **393**—Council of Hippo—Affirms canon of New Testament

* **397**—Council of Carthage—Affirms canon of New Testament

* **400**—Jerome completes the Latin Vulgate, a Greek manuscript containing the 39 books of the Old Testament, the 27 books of the New Testament, and the 14 books of the Apocrypha

* **995**—Anglo-Saxon (early roots of English language)

translations of the New Testament

- **1227**—Archbishop of Canterbury Cardinal Stephen Langdon believed to have divided Bible into chapters still used today.

- **1246**—Cardinal Hugo de Sancto Caro introduces system of Bible chapters

- **1384**—Death of John Wycliffe, who began the translation of the Bible (the 66 books in the canon of Scripture as well as the Apocrypha) into English. The work was completed after his death

- **c. 1455**—German inventor Johannes Gutenberg develops moveable-type printing press, allowing for mass production of books. The first book printed is the Gutenberg Bible

- **1516**—Dutch theologian Desiderius Erasmus produces Greek/Latin parallel New Testament

- **1522**—Martin Luther's German New Testament published

- **1526**—William Tyndale's complete New Testament, the first printed in English

- **1528**—Italian Dominican Bible scholar Santi Pagnini is the first to divide New Testament text into chapters and verses; his system was never widely adopted

- **1534**—Martin Luther's complete German translation published

- **1535**—Myles Coverdale's Bible, the first complete Bible printed in the English language

- **1537**—Matthew-Tyndale Bible, the second complete Bible printed in English. Done by John "Thomas Matthew" Rogers

- **1539**—The "Great Bible," the first English language Bible authorized for public use, printed

- **1551**—Printer Robert Estienne (Robertus Stephanus in Latin) adds verse notations to New Testament text

- **1557**—English scholar William Whittingham produces first English New Testament with verse divisions

- **1560**—The Geneva Bible, the first English language Bible to include both chapter and verse references, printed

- **1568**—The Bishops' Bible printed; revised substantially in 1572; the revised edition was the base text for the King James Version of 1611

- **1609**—The Douay Old Testament and the Rheims New Testament (produced in 1582) are combined to make the first complete English Catholic Bible

- **1611**—The King James Bible, including the Apocrypha, printed; Apocrypha was removed in 1885, leaving the 66 books we have today

- **1782**—Robert Aitken's Bible (King James Version), the first English language Bible printed in America

- **1885**—The "English Revised Version" Bible, the first major revision of the King James Version, published

- **1900**—American publishing company Thomas Nelson & Sons publishes the American Standard Version Old Testament; the following year, the company released the entire Bible, the first major American revision of the King James Bible

- **1952**—The Revised Standard Version published
- **1965**—The Amplified Bible published
- **1971**—The New American Standard Bible and The Living Bible published
- **1978**—The complete New International Version (NIV) published
- **1982**—The complete New King James Version published
- **1996**—The complete New Living Translation published
- **2002**—The complete The Message published
- **2004**—Holman Christian Standard Bible published

INTERESTING FACTS ABOUT THE KING JAMES BIBLE

- **First word in the Bible:** "In" (Genesis 1:1)
- **Last word in the Bible:** "Amen" (Revelation 22:21)
- **Least common words:** There are 14,565 words found only once in the King James Bible
- **Longest word in the Bible:** Mahershalalhashbaz, eighteen characters (Isaiah 8:1)
- **Longest non-name words in the Old Testament (16 characters):** evilfavouredness (Deuteronomy 17:1) and lovingkindness (several times)
- **Longest non-name words in the New Testament (16 characters):** covenantbreakers (Romans 1:31), fellow-prisoners (Romans 16:7), unprofitableness (Hebrews 7:18)
- **Surprising words you won't find in the Bible:** trinity, rapture, smile, evangelism
- **Midpoint books:** Micah and Nahum
- **Midpoint chapter:** Psalm 117
- **Midpoint verses:** Psalm 118:8

- **Shortest chapter (by number of words):** Psalm 117
- **Longest book:** Psalms (150 chapters)
- **Longest chapter:** Psalm 119 (176 verses)
- **Midpoint Old Testament book:** Proverbs
- **Midpoint Old Testament chapter:** Job 20
- **Midpoint Old Testament verses:** 2 Chronicles 20:17, 18
- **Shortest Old Testament book:** Obadiah
- **Shortest Old Testament verse:** 1 Chronicles 1:25
- **Longest Old Testament chapter:** Psalm 119
- **Midpoint New Testament book:** 2 Thessalonians
- **Midpoint New Testament chapters:** Romans 8–9
- **Midpoint New Testament verse:** Acts 27:17
- **Shortest New Testament book:** 3 John
- **Longest New Testament book:** Luke

THE BIBLE BY THE NUMBERS

- **Number of books:** 66 (39 in the Old Testament, 27 in the New)
- **Number of different writers:** 40
- **Number of chapters:** 1,189 (929 in the Old Testament, 260 in the New)
- **Number of verses:** 31,101
- **Number of words:** 783,137 to 788,280

- **Number of letters:** approximately 3,566,480
- **Longest book in the Old Testament:** Psalms (42,684 words)
- **Longest book in the New Testament:** Luke (25,939 words)
- **Shortest book in the Old Testament:** Obadiah (669 words)
- **Shortest book in the New Testament:** 3 John (294 words)
- **Shortest chapter in the Bible:** Psalm 117 (2 verses, 33 words)
- **Longest chapter in the Bible:** Psalm 119 (176 verses)
- **Promises:** approximately 1,260
- **Commands:** approximately 6,468
- **Predictions/prophecies:** more than 8,000
- **Fulfilled prophecies:** approximately 3,268 verses
- **Unfulfilled prophecies:** approximately 3,140
- **Number of questions:** 3,294
- **Different Hebrew words in the original manuscripts:** 8,674
- **Different Greek words in the original manuscripts:** 5,624
- **Different English words in the King James Version:** 12,143
- **Number of languages Bible has been translated into:** more than 1,200

- **Number of Bibles sold, given away, or distributed in the United States:** 168,000 daily

5 LONGEST VERSES IN THE BIBLE

1. **Esther 8:9**—Then were the king's scribes called at that time in the third month, that is, the month Sivan, on the three and twentieth day thereof; and it was written according to all that Mordecai commanded unto the Jews, and to the lieutenants, and the deputies and rulers of the provinces which are from India unto Ethiopia, an hundred twenty and seven provinces, unto every province according to the writing thereof, and unto every people after their language, and to the Jews according to their writing, and according to their language. (90 words)

2. **Jeremiah 21:7**—And afterward, saith the LORD, I will deliver Zedekiah king of Judah, and his servants, and the people, and such as are left in this city from the pestilence, from the sword, and from the famine, into the hand of Nebuchadrezzar king of Babylon, and into the hand of their enemies, and into the hand of those that seek their life: and he shall smite them with the edge of the sword; he shall not spare them, neither have pity, nor have mercy. (83 words)

3. **Joshua 8:33**—And all Israel, and their elders, and officers, and their judges, stood on this side the ark and on that side before the priests the Levites, which bare the ark of the covenant of the LORD, as well the stranger, as he that was born among them; half of

them over against mount Gerizim, and half of them over against mount Ebal; as Moses the servant of the LORD had commanded before, that they should bless the people of Israel. (80 words)

4. **Ezekiel 48:21**—And the residue shall be for the prince, on the one side and on the other of the holy oblation, and of the possession of the city, over against the five and twenty thousand of the oblation toward the east border, and westward over against the five and twenty thousand toward the west border, over against the portions for the prince: and it shall be the holy oblation; and the sanctuary of the house shall be in the midst thereof. (80 words)

5. **Jeremiah 44:12**—And I will take the remnant of Judah, that have set their faces to go into the land of Egypt to sojourn there, and they shall all be consumed, and fall in the land of Egypt; they shall even be consumed by the sword and by the famine: they shall die, from the least even unto the greatest, by the sword and by the famine: and they shall be an execration, and an astonishment, and a curse, and a reproach. (80 words)

11 SHORTEST VERSES IN THE BIBLE

There are several verses in the Old Testament that contain just a few words. For example, 1 Chronicles 1:25 reads, "Eber, Peleg, Reu." Here are the eleven shortest verses made up of actual sentences:

1. **John 11:35:** "Jesus wept" (2 words)

2. **1 Thessalonians 5:16:** "Rejoice evermore" (2 words)

3. **Luke 17:32:** "Remember Lot's wife" (3 words)

4. **1 Thessalonians 5:17:** "Pray without ceasing" (3 words)

5. **1 Thessalonians 5:20:** "Despise not prophesyings" (3 words)

6. **Exodus 20:13:** "Thou shalt not kill" (4 words)

7. **Exodus 20:15:** "Thou shalt not steal" (4 words)

8. **Deuteronomy 5:17:** "Thou shalt not kill" (4 words)

9. **Deuteronomy 5:19:** "Neither shalt thou steal" (4 words)

10. **1 Thessalonians 5:19:** "Quench not the Spirit" (4 words)

11. **1 Thessalonians 5:25:** "Brethren, pray for us" (4 words)

WORDS IN THE BIBLE

THE BIBLE'S TOP 20 MOST COMMONLY USED WORDS:

* **The:** approximately 64,040 times
* **And:** approximately 60,382 times
* **Of:** approximately 40,029 times
* **To:** approximately 16,372 times

- **That:** approximately 15,778 times
- **In:** approximately 14,482 times
- **He:** approximately 12,425 times
- **Shall:** approximately 10,939 times
- **For:** approximately 10,889 times
- **Unto:** approximately 10,100 times
- **A:** approximately 7,582 times

MOST COMMONLY USED NOUNS (PERSONS, PLACES, AND THINGS) IN THE BIBLE:

- **Lord:** approximately 7,970 times
- **God:** approximately 4,473 times
- **Man:** approximately 2,737 times
- **Israel:** approximately 2,576 times
- **King:** approximately 2,540 times
- **Son:** approximately 2,393 times
- **People:** approximately 2,143 times
- **House:** approximately 2,026 times
- **Day:** approximately 1,741 times
- **Men:** approximately 1,677 times

MOST COMMONLY USED
PEOPLE NAMES IN THE BIBLE:

- **David:** approximately 1,139 times
- **Jesus:** approximately 981 times
- **Moses:** approximately 848 times
- **Judah:** approximately 817 times
- **Jacob:** approximately 377 times
- **Saul:** approximately 425 times
- **Aaron:** approximately 350 times
- **Solomon:** approximately 306 times
- **Abraham:** approximately 250 times
- **Joseph:** approximately 250 times

MOST COMMONLY USED PLACE NAMES:

- **Israel:** approximately 2,575 times
- **Jerusalem:** approximately 814 times
- **Egypt:** approximately 610 times
- **Babylon:** approximately 295 times
- **Jordan:** approximately 190 times
- **Moab:** approximately 160 times
- **Samaria:** approximately 125 times
- **Assyria:** approximately 115 times
- **Gilead:** approximately 100 times
- **Canaan:** approximately 90 times

VERSES THAT CONTAIN ALL BUT
ONE LETTER OF THE ENGLISH ALPHABET:

- Ezra 7:21 (all but j)
- Joshua 7:24 (all but q)
- 1 Kings 1:9 (all but q)
- 1 Chronicles 12:40 (all but q)
- 2 Chronicles 36:10 (all but q)
- Ezekiel 28:13 (all but q)
- Daniel 4:37 (all but q)
- Haggai 1:1 (all but q)
- 2 Kings 16:15 (all but z)
- 1 Chronicles 4:10 (all but z)
- Galatians 1:14 (all but k)

3 | THE BIBLE AS HISTORY: IMPORTANT TIMES, PEOPLE, AND EVENTS

TIMELINE OF IMPORTANT BIBLICAL EVENTS

- **c. 4000 BC**—The Fall
- **c. 2350 BC**—The Flood
- **c. 2235 BC**—Dispersion of the races
- **c. 2100–1500 BC**—Age of the Patriarchs (Middle Bronze Age)
- **c. 1950 BC**—Amorites conquer Mesopotamia
- **c. 1925 BC**—Call of Abraham
- **c. 1720 BC**—Joseph becomes governor of Egypt
- **c. 1635 BC**—Joseph's death
- **c. 1575 BC**—Birth of Moses
- **c. 1500–1200 BC**—Exodus and Promised Land Conquest (Late Bronze Age)
- **c. 1492 BC**—The Exodus from Egypt
- **c. 1452 BC**—Joshua appointed leader of the people of Israel
- **c. 1451 BC**—The crossing of the Jordan
- **c. 1451–44 BC**—Conquest of Canaan

- **c. 1394–1095 BC**—The period of the Judges
- **c. 1095–1055 BC**—King Saul, Israel's first monarch
- **c. 1055–1015 BC**—King David
- **c. 1050 BC**—Philistines settle in southern Palestine
- **c. 1015–975 BC**—King Solomon
- **c. 1005 BC**—Dedication of the Temple
- **c. 975–587 BC**—The divided kingdom (Judah and Israel)
- **c. 721 BC**—Captivity of Israel
- **c. 587 BC**—Babylonian Captivity of Judah
- **c. 535 BC**—Return of the Jews to Jerusalem under Zerubbabel
- **c. 515 BC**—Second Temple dedicated
- **c. 458 BC**—Ezra leads second wave of Jews back to Jerusalem
- **c. 445 BC**—Nehemiah returns to Jerusalem and begins rebuilding city walls
- **c. 37 BC–AD 4**—Reign of Herod the Great, Roman-appointed king of Judea
- **c. 4 BC–AD 6**—Rule of Herod Archelaus, ethnarch of Judea, Samaria, and Idumea
- **c. 4 BC–AD 39**—Rule of Herod Antipas, tetrarch of Galilee and Perea
- **c. 4 BC–AD 34**—Rule of Herod Philip, tetrarch of Iturea and Trachonitis

- **c. 4–6 BC**—Birth of Jesus Christ
- **c. 2 BC**—Birth of Saul of Tarsus (Later, the apostle Paul)
- **c. AD 20**—Reconstruction of the Temple begins
- **c. AD 25–28**—Ministry of John the Baptist
- **c. AD 25–27**—Christ's baptism
- **c. AD 26–37**—Pontius Pilate prefect of Judea
- **c. AD 29–30**—Christ's crucifixion & resurrection
- **c. AD 31–37**—Conversion of Saul of Tarsus (the apostle Paul)
- **c. AD 31–95**—Books of the New Testament written
- **c. AD 41**—Execution of James by Herod Agrippa I
- **c. AD 45–58**—The apostle Paul's missionary journeys
- **c. AD 49**—Roman Emperor Claudius expels Jews from Rome; the church holds the Council of Jerusalem
- **c. AD 54**—Nero becomes Roman emperor
- **c. AD 59–60**—Paul's first imprisonment begins
- **c. AD 62**—Execution of James, the Lord's brother, in Jerusalem
- **c. AD 67–68**—Paul's final imprisonment and death in Rome
- **AD 70**—Jerusalem captured by Titus; Herod's Temple destroyed
- **AD 81**—Domitian becomes Roman emperor
- **AD 90–100**—Persecution of Christians by Domitian
- **AD 90–100**—Death of the apostle John, the last living apostle

THE LIVES OF SIX MOST IMPORTANT BIBLICAL FIGURES

ABRAHAM

* **From Ur of the Chaldees to Haran**—The death of his father, Terah (Genesis 11:31–32)

* **From Haran to Shechem**—Builds altar (Genesis 12:1–7)

* **From Shechem to Bethel**—Abraham and Lot offer sacrifices to God (Genesis 12:8)

* **From Bethel to Egypt**—Abraham denies Sarah is his wife (Genesis 12:10–16)

* **From Egypt to Bethel**—Abraham offers prayers (Genesis 13:1–4)

* **From Bethel to Hebron**—Builds altar and offers sacrifice (Genesis 13:18)

* **From Hebron to Horab**—Abraham rescues Lot (Genesis 14:1–16)

* **From Horab to Hebron**—Ishmael born; three angels give promise of a son; Sodom destroyed (Genesis 14:16–19:25)

* **From Hebron to Gerar**—Isaac born and presented to Abraham (Genesis 20:1–21:16)

* **From Gerar to Beersheba**—Abraham makes covenant with Abimelech (Genesis 21:31–33:33)

* **From Beersheba to Mt. Moriah**—Abraham willing to sacrifice Isaac but is stopped from doing so at the last moment (Genesis 22:1–18)

- **From Mt. Moriah to Beersheba** (Genesis 22:19)

- **From Beersheba to Hebron**—The death of his wife, Sarah (Genesis 23:1–2, 19–20)

- **From Hebron to Beersheba**—The death of Abraham at 175 years of age (Genesis 25:7–8)

- **Isaac and Ishmael** carry Abraham's body to Hebron (Genesis 25:9)

MOSES

- **Family**—Father Amram, mother Jochebed (Exodus 6:20); from the tribe of Levi (Exodus 2:1); brother Aaron (Exodus 4:14) and sister Miriam (Exodus 15:20)

- **Early Life (Exodus 2:2–10)**—His birth; hidden in the reeds, adopted by king's daughter, and named Moses

- **Youth and Adulthood (Exodus 2:11–15)**—Kills an Egyptian and flees to Midian

- **At Midian (Exodus 2:16–25)**—Marries Zipporah, a priest's daughter

- **God's Call—(Exodus 3:1–4:16)**—Moses sees burning bush and hears God's call but makes excuses; God promises divine and human help

- **Return to Egypt (Exodus 4:29–12:29)**—Demands that a stubborn Pharaoh free the people of Israel; God sends plagues; the Passover established; Pharaoh frees Israelites

- **The Exodus from Egypt (Exodus 12:30–18:27)**—
  Pharaoh pursues the Israelites; the crossing of the Red
  Sea; the Song of Moses; God provides for the Israelites

- **At Mount Sinai (Exodus 19:1–40:1–38)**—Moses
  ascends the mountain three times and makes
  covenant with God; receives the Ten Commandments
  and the rest of the Law; the golden calf

- **Journey from Sinai to Kadesh Barnea (Numbers
  10:11–12:15)**—The pillar of cloud; the people
  complain; seventy elders appointed

- **At Kadesh Barnea (Numbers 13:26–14:45)**—The
  spies' report on the Promised Land; the people rebel,
  resulting in God's wrath; Amelek defeats Israel

- **Forty Years in the Wilderness (Numbers 14:33–
  16:50)**—God declares the people would wander;
  rebellion breaks out

- **Return to Kadesh Barnea (Numbers 20:1–13)**—The
  death of Miriam, Moses' sister; the people complain
  over lack of water; Moses' sin

- **Journey to the Jordan River (Numbers 20:14–
  33:49)**—The death of Aaron; the fiery serpents; the
  story of Balaam

- **Moses' Final Days (Deuteronomy
  32:1–34:6)**—Moses' farewell address and blessing;
  Moses views Promised Land; Moses' death

- **Appearance at the Transfiguration (Matthew
  17:3)**—Moses and Elijah appear at Jesus'
  transfiguration

JOSHUA

*   **At the Wilderness of Paran (Numbers 13–14)**—One of the twelve spies to spy out the land of Canaan; of the twelve, only he and Caleb gave an encouraging report

*   **In Moab (Numbers 27:18–23)**—Moses chooses Joshua to assume leadership

*   **Mt. Nebo (Deuteronomy 37:7–14)**—Joshua ordained as Moses' successor

*   **Shittim (Joshua 1:1–11)**—God's words of instruction and encouragement

*   **From Shittim to the Jordan (Joshua 1:10–18; 3:1–3)**—Joshua assembles leaders and gives them instructions for the crossing of the Jordan River

*   **Spies sent to Jericho and hidden by Rahab (2:1–24)**

*   **Crossing the Jordan (Joshua 3–4)**—The people of Israel cross the river on dry ground; twelve men bring stones from the riverbed for a memorial at Gilgal

*   **From Gilgal to Jericho (Joshua 5:13–6:27)**—God promises to help Joshua; Jericho captured and destroyed; Rahab and her family spared

*   **From Jericho to Ai (Joshua 7:1–8:29)**—Achan's sin leads to defeat; Achan is punished for his disobedience; Israel returns to Jericho; Israel destroys Ai in second attempt

*   **From Ai to Mt. Ebal (Joshua 8:30–35)**—Altar erected and Law read

- **From Ebal to Gibeon (Joshua 9:1–10:15)**—Joshua tricked by the Gibeonites; Israel defends Gibeon, and the sun stands still

- **In Makkedah (Joshua 10:16–27)**—Five kings defeated

- **Southern Campaign (Joshua 10:20–43)**—From Makkedah to Libnah, Lichish, Gezer, Eglon, Hebron, Debir, Kadesh Barnea, Goshen, Gaza, and surrounding countries

- **Northern Campaign (Joshua 11:1–15)**—Sidon, Hazor, and other cities routed

- **Division of the Land (Joshua 13:8–21:45)**—Temple erected and tribes allotted their share of the land

- **At Shechem, Joshua's Farewell Address (Joshua 23–24)**—Joshua and Israel renew their covenant with God

- **Joshua's Death at 110 Years of Age (Joshua 24:29–32)**—Joshua's bones buried at Shechem

DAVID

- **Early (1 Samuel 16:1–13)**—Samuel anoints David as King

- **Between Jerusalem and Gibeah (1 Samuel 16:14–23, 17:15)**—A harpist for King Saul

- **From Bethlehem to Elah to Gibeah (1 Samuel 17:26–58)**—David confronts and slays the giant warrior Goliath; carries the giant's head to Gibeah

- **Between Gibeah and Jerusalem (1 Samuel 18:1–19:10)**—David given a high rank in Saul's army; Saul is jealous of David and attempts to kill him with a spear; David attacks the Philistines and kills 200; again sent out to fight the Philistines, but Saul tries again to kill him when he returns

- **From Gibeah to Ramah to Naioth to Gibeah (1 Samuel 19:18–21:42)**—David flees to Samuel the prophet at Ramah; when he returns to Gibeah, Saul's son Jonathan alerts him of Saul's plan to kill David

- **From Gibeah to Nob to Gath (1 Samuel 21:1–15)**—Ahimelech gives David consecrated bread and the sword of Goliath; David feigns insanity in Gath; Saul kills the priests of Gath

- **From Gath to Adullam to Mizpah to the Forest of Hereth to Keila (1 Samuel 22:1–5)**—Removes his parents from danger in Mizpah; fights the Philistines in Keila

- **From Keilah to the Desert of Ziph to the Desert of Moan to En Gedi to the Desert of Moan (1 Samuel 21:14–29)**—Forms a lasting allegiance with Jonathan in Ziph; spares Saul's life in En Gedi

- **From the Desert of Moan to Carmel (1 Samuel 25–26)**—Meets and marries Abigail, Nabal's widow; again spares Saul's life

- **From the Desert of Moan and Carmel to Gath to Ziklag to Gath (1 Samuel 27:1–9)**—Conquers the Geshurites, the Girzites, and Amelekites

- **From Gath to Aphek to Ziklag to the south (1 Samuel 29:9–30:26)**—Finds Ziklag ravaged by the Amalekites; travels south to recover the property of the people of Ziklag; returns to Ziklag

- **From Ziklag to Hebron (2 Samuel 5:1–3)**—Anointed king of Israel following the death of Saul and Jonathan

- **From Hebron to Jerusalem to Baal Perazim to Jerusalem (2 Samuel 3:1–5:21)**—Drives Philistines out of Baal Perazim and returns to Jerusalem

- **From Jerusalem to Rephaim (2 Samuel 5:22–25)**—Drives Philistines from Rephaim to Geba and Gezer

- **From Jerusalem to Baalah to Gibeah (2 Samuel 6:2–11)**—Goes to bring the ark of the covenant back to Jerusalem, but leaves it on Nachon's threshing floor

- **From Jerusalem to the house of Obed-Edom (2 Samuel 6:14–23)**—Brings the ark back to Jerusalem; his wife, Michal, unhappy with his dancing before the Lord

- **From Jerusalem to Metheg Ammah to Moab to Zobah to the Valley of Salt (2 Samuel 8:1–13)**—Conquers Metheg Ammah; places Moab under his control; conquers Hadadezer in Zobath; kills 18,000 Edomites at the Valley of Salt

- **From Jerusalem to Helam (2 Samuel 10:17–19)**—Conquers the Arameans

- **Jerusalem (2 Samuel 11)**—David's sin with Bathsheba

- **From Jerusalem to Rabbah (2 Samuel 12:29–31)**—

Inhabitants of Rabbah are treated with cruelty

- **From Jerusalem to Mahanaim (2 Samuel 15–17)**—Flees to Mahanaim following his son Absalom's coup; returns to Jerusalem and resumes the throne after Absalom's death

- **From Jerusalem to Jabesh Gilead (2 Samuel 21:12–14)**—Returns bones of Saul and Jonathan back to the land of Benjamin for burial in their father's tomb

- **From Jerusalem for final battle with Philistines**—Place of battle unknown; Ishbi-Benob wanted to kill David

- **Jerusalem (1 Kings 2:1–11)**—Before his death, David instructs his son and successor, Solomon

JESUS

HIS EARLY LIFE
(MATTHEW 1:1–2:23; LUKE 1:1–2:52)

- **Angel visits Mary** (Luke 1:26–38)
- **Birth of John the Baptist** (Luke 1:5–22, 57–80)
- **Birth of Jesus** (Luke 2:1–7)
- **The shepherds' visit** (Luke 2:8–17)
- **Presentation at the temple** (Luke 2:22–38)
- **Visit of the magi** (Matthew 2:1–12)
- **Escape to Egypt** (Matthew 2:13–15)

- **Return to Nazareth** (Matthew 2:19–23; Luke 2:39)
- **Visit to temple at 12 years old** (Luke 2:41–50)

FIRST YEAR OF MINISTRY

- **Baptized by John the Baptist** (Matthew 3:1–17; Mark 1:1–11; Luke 3:1–22)
- **The temptation** (Matthew 4:1–11; Mark 1:12–13; Luke 4:1–13)
- **Testimony of John the Baptist** (John 1:19–36)
- **Conversation with Nicodemus** (John 3:1–21)
- **Cleansed temple** (John 2:13–17)
- **First miracle, water to wine** (John 2:13–25)
- **Water of life conversation with Samaritan woman** (John 4:4–26)
- **Taught in Nazareth, rejected** (Luke 4:16–30)

SECOND YEAR OF MINISTRY

- **Sermon on the Mount** (Matthew 5–7; Luke 6:20–49)
- **Twelve apostles ordained** (Matthew 10:1–4; Mark 3:13–19; Luke 6:12–16)
- **Faced opposition** (Matthew 12:14–25; Mark 3:6, 22–27; Luke 6:11–15, 17–23)
- **Healed the sick** (Matthew 8:2–4, 14–15; 9:20–22; Mark 1:29–31, 40–41; 5:25; 34; Luke 4:38–39, 8:43–48)

- **Freed the demon-possessed** (Matthew 8:28–34, 12:22; Mark 1:23–28, 5:1–20; Luke 4:33–37, 8:26–39, 11:14)
- **Raised the dead** (Luke 7:12–16; Matthew 9:18–26; Mark 5:22–43; Luke 8:43–48)
- **Taught in parables** (Matthew 13:3–51; Mark 8:14–15, 12:36–13:21; Luke 7:41–43, 12:16–13:21)
- **Calmed a storm** (Matthew 8:24–27; Mark 4:37–41; Luke 8:23–25)

THIRD YEAR OF MINISTRY

- **Feeds 5,000** (Matthew 14:15–21; Mark 6:35–44; Luke 9:12–17; John 6:5–14)
- **Walks on water** (Matthew 14:22–33; Mark 6:45–52; John 6:16–21)
- **Bread of life** (John 6:25–29)
- **Feeds 4,000** (Matthew 15:32–38; Mark 8:1–9)
- **Peter confesses Him as the Christ** (Matthew 16:13–19; Mark 8:27–29; Luke 9:18–21)
- **Performs many miracles** (Matthew 14:34–36, 15:29–31; Mark 6:53–56)
- **The transfiguration** (Matthew 17:1–9; Mark 9:2–10; Luke 9:28–36)
- **Foretells suffering** (Matthew 17:22–28; Mark 9:30–32; Luke 9:43–45)
- **Parable of the good Samaritan** (Luke 10:25–37)

- **Raises Lazarus from the dead** (John 11:1–46)

THE FINAL MONTHS

- **Teaches in parables** (Luke 14:15–16:31, 18:1–14, 19:11–27)
- **Heals the sick** (Luke 13:10–17, 14:1–6; Matthew 20:29–34)
- **The second coming of Christ** (Luke 17:20–37)
- **The rich young man** (Matthew 19:16–30; Mark 10:17–31; Luke 18:18–30)
- **Foretells sufferings again** (Matthew 20:17–19; Mark 10:32–34; Luke 18:31–34)
- **Anointed at Bethany** (Matthew 26:6–13; Mark 14:3–9; John 12:2–8)

THE FINAL WEEK

- **Triumphal entry into Jerusalem** (Matthew 21:1–11; Mark 11:1–11; Luke 19:29–44; John 12:12–19
- **Cleanses the temple** (Matthew 21:12–13; Mark 11:15–17; Luke 19:45–46)
- **Coming events** (Matthew 24:15–42; Mark 13:14–37; Luke 21:20–36)
- **Teaches in parables** (Matthew 21:28–22:14; 25:1–30)
- **The plot of the Jews and Judas** (Matthew 26:1–16; Mark 14:1–72; Luke 22:1–6)

- **Washes disciples' feet** (John 13:1–17)
- **The Lord's Supper** (Matthew 26:26–29; Mark 14:22–25; Luke 22:19–20)
- **Parting words** (John 14:1–31)
- **Promise of the Holy Spirit** (John 16:7–15)
- **Prays for His followers** (John 17:1–26)
- **In the garden of Gethsemane** (Matthew 26:36–46; Mark 14:32–42; Luke 22:39–46; John 18:1)
- **Betrayal by Judas** (Matthew 26:47–56; Mark 14:43–52; Luke 22:47–53; John 18:3–13)
- **Jesus before the authorities** (Matthew 26:58–27:14; Mark 14:55–15:5; Luke 22:66–23:12; John 18:19–40)

HIS DEATH AND RESURRECTION

- **The crucifixion** (Matthew 27:35–38; Mark 15:25–28; Luke 23:33–38; John 19:18–24)
- **His death** (Matthew 27:45–50; Mark 15:33–37; Luke 23:44–46; John 19:28–30)
- **His burial** (Matthew 27:59–61; Mark 15:46–47; Luke 23:53; John 19:39–42)
- **Mary finds empty tomb** (John 20:2)
- **Jesus appears to Mary Magdalene** (Mark 16:9; John 20:11–17)
- **Jesus appears to the other women** (Matthew 28:8–10)
- **Jesus appears to Peter** (Luke 24:34)

- **Jesus appears to the Eleven** (Mark 16:14–18; John 20:26–29)
- **His ascension to heaven** (Mark 16:19–20; Luke 24:50–53; Acts 1:4–9)

THE APOSTLE PAUL

HIS LIFE BEFORE BECOMING AN APOSTLE

- **Born in Tarsus** (Acts 23:3)
- **A pharisee himself and son of a pharisee** (Acts 23:6)
- **Studied under the Jewish teacher Gamaliel** (Acts 22:3)
- **Citizen of Rome** (Acts 22:25–28)
- **Sister lived in Jerusalem** (Acts 23:6)
- **Chief persecutor of the early church** (Acts 9:1–3, 22:4)
- **Present at the stoning of Stephen** (Acts 7:58)
- **Converted near Damascus** (Acts 9:3–18)

C. AD 45–48—FIRST MISSIONARY JOURNEY (ACTS 13–14), WITH BARNABAS

- **Departs from Antioch, Syria** (13:1–3)
- **Cyprus, home of Barnabas** (13:4–12)
- **Perga (13:13)**—John Mark leaves them
- **Pisidian Antioch (13:14–41)**—First Gentile Christian congregation

- **Iconium (13:51–14:6)**—Many believe; Paul and his companions flee for Lystra and Derbe when they learn of a plan to stone them

- **Lystra (14:8–19)**—Paul and Barnabas treated as gods; later stoned

- **Derbe (14:20–21)**—Many new disciples of Christ

- **Return to Syrian Antioch (14:21–26)**—On the way home, they appoint elders at churches in Lystra, Iconium, and Pisidian Antioch

C. AD 50–53—Second Missionary Journey, with Silas (Acts 15:36–18:22)

- **Departure from Antioch, Syria (15:36–40)**—Paul and Barnabas separate over disagreement over John Mark. Paul selects Silas to travel with him

- **Syria and Cilicia (15:41)**—Encourages the churches there

- **Derbe and Lystra (16:1–3)**—Timothy joins the group

- **Phrygia & Galatia (16:6)**—Holy Spirit prevents them going to Bithynia

- **Troas (16:9)**—Paul has vision of Macedonian man; Luke apparently joins them (16:10)

- **Philippi (16:13–34)**—Conversion of Lydia and her family; Paul and Silas beaten and imprisoned; earthquake and conversion of jailer

- **Thessalonica (17:4)**—Thessalonian church founded

- **Berea (17:11–12)**—Jews receive the word and

examine scriptures to see if what Paul told them was true; many believe

- **Athens (17:16–33)**—Paul preaches the "Unknown God" on the Areopagus

- **Corinth (18:1–18)**—Stays for 18 months with Aquila and Priscilla, who later travel with him; writes 1 and 2 Thessalonians

- **Ephesus (18:19–20)**—A brief visit; leave Aquila and Priscilla there

- **Jerusalem (18:21–22)**—For a feast, possibly Pentecost

- **Return to Antioch (18:22)**

C. AD 53–58—THIRD MISSIONARY JOURNEY, WITH TIMOTHY (ACTS 18:23–28:31)

- **Phrygia and Galatia (18:23)**
- **Ephesus (19)**—Stays for two and one-half years; workers riot; writes 1 Corinthians and possibly Galatians
- **Macedonia & Greece (20:1–2)**—Writes 2 Corinthians
- **Troas (20:6–12)**—Stays for 7 days, preaches long sermon; raises Eutychus from the dead
- **Assos (20:13–14)**—Aristotle taught here
- **Ephesus (20:17–35)**— Farewell speech to Ephesian elders

- **Tyre (21:1–4)**—Stays seven days
- **Ptolemais (21:7)**—Stays one day
- **Caesarea (21:8)**—Stays with Philip the evangelist

IN JERUSALEM

- **Welcomed by the church** (Acts 21:17)
- **Taken by the Jews** (Acts 21:27–30)
- **His defense in Jerusalem** (Acts 22:1–21)
- **Taken by the Romans** (Acts 22:24–29)
- **Defense before the Sanhedrin** (23:1–10)
- **The plot to kill him** (Acts 23:12–15)

IN CAESAREA

- **His defense before Felix, governor of Judea** (Acts 24:10–21)
- **Imprisoned for two years** (Acts 24:27)
- **Appeals to Caesar** (Acts 25:10–12)
- **Defense before Agrippa** (Acts 26:1–29)

TAKEN TO ROME

- **Shipwreck** (Acts 27:14–28:10)
- **Arrival at Rome** (Acts 28:16)
- **Preaches in Rome** (Acts 28:30–31)
- **Paul's final words** (2 Timothy 4:6–8)

50 OF THE BIBLE'S MOST IMPORTANT PEOPLE

1 **Aaron**—Older brother of Moses, he was called into God's service when Moses balked at confronting Pharaoh over his enslavement of the people of Israel. "I know that he can speak well," God said of Aaron (Exodus 4:14). He became God's spokesman in support of Moses' leadership for nearly forty years. He was the first priest of Israel and headed a family line of priests that continued for more than a thousand years.

2 **Abraham**—The new name for Abram, whom God called out of Ur of the Chaldees and into the Promised Land. This new name was a symbol of the covenant between God and Abraham. The Lord promised to build a nation through Abraham and his wife, Sarai (whom he renamed Sarah), though she was too old to have children. God refused to accept Ishmael, son of Abraham and Sarah's maid, Hagar, as the child of promise. In time, God gave Sarah and Abraham a son, Isaac, who would found the nation God promised.

3 **Adam**—The first man, created by God to have dominion over the earth. Adam's first act was to

name the animals; then God created Adam's wife, Eve, as "an help meet for him" (Genesis 2:18). God gave this couple the beautiful Garden of Eden to care for. There Satan, in the form of a serpent, tempted Eve. God had banned them from eating the fruit of the knowledge of good and evil, but under Satan's influence Eve picked it, ate it, and offered it to Adam, who also ate.

4   **Barnabas**—A Cypriot Christian who sold some land and gave the profit to the church. After Saul's conversion, Barnabas introduced this previous persecutor of the church to the apostles and spoke up for him. When the Jerusalem church heard that Gentiles of Antioch had been converted, they sent Barnabas, who became one of the "prophets and teachers" at that church. Saul and Barnabas were sent on a missionary journey together.

5   **Cyrus**—The king of Persia who commanded that the temple in Jerusalem be rebuilt. He ordered all his people to give donations to help the Jews, and he returned the temple vessels that Nebuchadnezzar of Babylon had taken. When opposers objected to the work, the Jews reminded them of Cyrus's command, and the work went forward again. The prophet Daniel also lived and prospered during the early part of Cyrus's reign.

6   **Daniel**—An Old Testament major prophet. As a child, Daniel was taken into exile in Babylon. Because he refused to defile himself with meat and wine from the king's table, God blessed him with

knowledge and wisdom. Daniel interpreted a dream for Nebuchadnezzar, and the king made him ruler over the province of Babylon. Daniel interpreted a second dream for Nebuchadnezzar, predicting his downfall until he worshiped the Lord. During King Belshazzar's reign, Daniel interpreted the meaning of the mysterious handwriting on the wall. For this he was made third ruler in the kingdom, but Belshazzar died that night.

7   **David**—Popular king of Israel. As a young shepherd and musician, David was anointed king by the prophet Samuel in disobedient King Saul's place. David vanquished the Philistine giant, Goliath. Following a battle with the Philistines and the deaths of Saul and his sons, David was anointed king of Judah. Later, he also became king of Israel. David wrote many of the psalms and sang a song of praise about the victories God brought him (2 Samuel 22). Despite his failings, scripture refers to David as a man after God's own heart (Acts 13:22).

8   **Elijah**—An Old Testament prophet from Tishbe, in Gilead. His prophecy that no rain would fall in Israel, except at his command, angered wicked King Ahab, and Elijah had to flee across the Jordan River and on to Zarephath. God hid him for three years then sent him to Mount Carmel. At Carmel, Elijah had a showdown with the priests of Baal that proved the Lord was God. Baal could not ignite the offering made by the pagans, but God sent fire from heaven that lit Elijah's water-soaked offering. The people of

Israel worshiped God, and rain fell.

9   **Elisabeth**—Wife of the priest Zacharias and mother
of John the Baptist. For many years Elisabeth had
been barren, but her husband received a vision
promising she would conceive. When Elisabeth
heard, she rejoiced at God's favor. Her cousin Mary
visited her for three months when Mary learned she
would bear the Messiah.

10 **Elisha**—The prophet Elijah's successor and disciple,
Elisha saw Elijah carried up to heaven on a whirlwind
of fire and received a double portion of his spirit.
Elisha performed many miracles—he healed a
polluted water source for the people of Jericho,
provided oil for a widow, and caused a "great woman"
of Shunem to have a child, then brought him
back to life after he died. He fed a hundred people
from twenty loaves of bread. At Elisha's command,
Naaman, captain of the Syrian king, bathed in the
Jordan and was healed of leprosy.

11 **Esther**—The Jewish wife of the Persian king
Ahasuerus. Angered by his wife Vashti, the king
sought a new bride from among the most beautiful
women of his kingdom. As a result of this search, he
found Esther, fell in love with her, married her, and
made her his queen. Ahasuerus's favorite counselor,
Haman, lied to the king and plotted to kill the Jewish
people. Esther confronted her husband concerning
the plot. Angered, Ahasuerus had Haman killed, and
Esther and her people were saved.

12 **Eve**—Adam's wife, "the mother of all living" (Genesis
3:20). Tempted by the serpent, Eve ate the fruit of the
tree of the knowledge of good and evil and offered
it to her husband, who also ate. Suddenly fearful of
God because of their sin, they hid from Him. God
placed a curse on Adam and Eve. Eve would suffer
greatly during childbirth, desire her husband, and be
ruled over by him. God removed the couple from the
Garden of Eden. Three of their children were named
in the Bible—Cain and Abel, and after Cain murdered
Abel, God gave them another child, Seth. Genesis 5:4
says they had "many other sons and daughters."

13 **Ezra**—An Israelite scribe and teacher of the law who
returned from the Babylonian Exile along with some
priests, Levites, temple servants, and other Israelites.
Ezra had received the backing of King Artaxerxes
of Persia and returned with money and the temple
vessels. Ezra also had the right to appoint magistrates
and judges in Israel. When they reached Jerusalem,
the officials told Ezra that many men of Israel had
intermarried with the people around them and
followed their ways. Ezra prayed for the people, read
them the law, and called them to confess their sin.

14 **Gideon**—The fifth judge of Israel, whom God raised
up to lead his nation against the Midianites. The angel
of the Lord appeared to Gideon when he was hiding
his threshing from the enemy, told him God was with
him, and called him a "mighty man of valour" (Judges
6:12). Gideon's many doubts did not keep him from
obeying God. He made an offering, then tore down

the altar to Baal and cut down its grove, for which the men of his town wanted to kill him.

15 **Hannah**—Hannah could not bear a child, but her husband, Elkanah, loved her, though his second wife abused her. Distraught, Hannah went to the temple to pray and promised God that if He gave her a child, she would give the boy to Him for his whole life. As she fervently prayed, Eli the priest mistook her praying for drunkenness; then he discovered how wrong he had been. In time, Hannah conceived and bore Samuel. When he was weaned, the couple brought the boy to Eli to foster. Samuel became a powerful prophet of Israel.

16 **Hezekiah**—King of Judah who did right in God's eyes. Hezekiah removed pagan worship from the kingdom and kept God's commandments. Under his command, the Levites cleansed the temple and restored worship. When the Assyrian King Sennacherib attacked Judah, Hezekiah gave him a large tribute. Sennacherib sent officials to confer with Hezekiah's aides and try to convince his people to side with Sennacherib against their king and God. Sennacherib sent a message to Hezekiah belittling God and threatening Judah. Hezekiah brought the letter before God and asked Him to save Judah. Again, Isaiah prophesied the Assyrians' fall.

17 **Hosea**—A minor prophet whom God commanded to marry a prostitute, Gomer. She took a lover and ran from Hosea. God told Hosea to go to her and win her back. The prophet's tumultuous family life paralleled

the unfaithfulness of the people of Israel, who had
abandoned their covenant with God.

18 **Isaac**—The son of Abraham and Sarah whom God
promised to the long-barren couple. God tested
Abraham by commanding him to sacrifice Isaac at
Moriah. At the site of sacrifice, Abraham built an
altar and placed his son atop it. But the angel of the
Lord stopped the sacrifice, and God provided a ram
instead. Isaac married Rebekah, but she had trouble
conceiving, so Isaac prayed for a child. She bore two
sons, Esau and Jacob.

19 **Isaiah**—A prophet of Jerusalem who served during
the last year of the reign of King Uzziah and
the reigns of Jotham, Ahaz, and Hezekiah. This
aristocratic prophet was married to a prophetess and
had at least two children. Isaiah warned Ahaz of an
attack by Syria and warned against making treaties
with foreign nations. Also called "Esaias."

20 **Jacob**—Isaac and Rebekah's son who was born
clinging to the heel of his twin brother, Esau. Years
later, when the exhausted hunter, Esau, came home
and asked Jacob for his lentil stew, Jacob offered to
sell it to him for his birthright. Esau accepted. Later,
tricked by Laban, Jacob married both his daughters,
Leah and his beloved Rachel. From them and their
handmaids, Bilhah and Zilpah, Jacob had twelve sons,
founders of Israel's twelve tribes. He was later renamed
Israel and began to understand God's deliverance.

21 **James**—Jesus' brother, called James the less (younger).
When the people of the synagogue were astonished at

Jesus' teachings, they asked if this was not the brother of James. James became a leader in the Jerusalem church. Paul visited him after returning from Arabia. When he saw that Paul had received God's grace, James and some other disciples accepted him for ministry. This James is believed by many to be the writer of the book of James in the New Testament.

22 **Jeremiah**—A prophet of Judah during the reigns of kings Josiah, Jehoahaz, Jehoiakim, Jehoiachin, and Zedekiah. Following Assyria's destruction of Israel, Babylon threatened Judah. The turmoil of his age was clearly reflected in the gloomy prophecies of Jeremiah. He condemned Judah for idolatry and called the nation to repentance. God warned of Judah's destruction and mourned over it, yet Jerusalem refused to repent, and Jeremiah warned of the coming judgment. He wrote the books of Jeremiah and Lamentations.

23 **Jesus**—God's Son and humanity's Savior, Jesus existed from the beginning. Through the Holy Spirit He became incarnated within the womb of Mary and was born in a humble Bethlehem stable. He grew up in Nazareth, learning the carpentry trade of His earthly father, Joseph. Jesus began His ministry when He was about thirty. Following an illegal trial, Jesus died for humanity's sin on the cross. After His resurrection, He appeared to Mary Magdalene and then the disciples and others. He appeared to the faithful for forty days, then commissioned the apostles to spread the Good News and ascended to heaven.

24 **Job**—A righteous man from the land of Uz whom
God tested to prove to Satan that Job was not faithful
to Him because he had many physical blessings. For
a time, God gave Job into Satan's power. First Job lost
his cattle and servants. Then a messenger came with
news that all his children had been killed. Yet Job
worshiped God. Satan covered Job with sores, and his
wife told him, "Curse God, and die" (Job 2:9). Yet he
remained faithful. Eventually, God restored all of Job's
original blessings.

25 **John**—A son of Zebedee and brother of James,
John became Jesus' disciple when the Master called
the brothers to leave their fishing boat and follow
Him. Describing himself in his gospel as the disciple
whom Jesus loved, John indicated their intimate
relationship. As his closest disciples, he, James, and
Peter experienced events such as the healings of
Peter's mother-in-law and Jairus's daughter and the
transfiguration of Jesus. John wrote the gospel and
letters that bear his name and the book of Revelation.

26 **John the Baptist**—John was Jesus' cousin. He was
born to the elderly couple Zacharias and Elisabeth
after an angel told the doubtful Zacharias of the
birth, then temporarily struck him dumb for unbelief.
Before Jesus began His ministry, John preached a
message of repentance in the desert and, in the Jordan
River, baptized those who confessed their sins. He
also confronted the Pharisees and Sadducees with
their lack of repentance. John foretold that another
more worthy than he would baptize with the Holy

Spirit. He unwillingly baptized Jesus and saw the Spirit of God descend on Him.

27 **Jonah**—An Old Testament minor prophet whom God commanded to preach in Nineveh, home of Israel's Assyrian enemies. Fearing God would give mercy to his enemies, Jonah fled on a ship headed for Tarshish. When a tempest struck the ship, the sailors threw Jonah overboard. Jonah was swallowed by a fish. When he praised God, the fish vomited him onto land. Jonah went to Nineveh and preached, and the people repented. The angry prophet, wanting to die, fled the city. God pointed out that Jonah had more compassion for a plant that died than for the people of the city.

28 **Joseph (the Patriarch)**—Son of Jacob and Rachel. Joseph was Jacob's favorite son, which made his other sons jealous. Joseph angered his brothers when he told them he would one day rule over them. They threw him into an empty pit, then sold him to some passing traders. Carried to Egypt, Joseph became slave to the captain of Pharaoh's guard. After the captain's wife accused him of trying to seduce her, Joseph landed in prison, where he interpreted the dreams of two of Pharaoh's servants. Given an opportunity to interpret Pharaoh's dream, he became second in command in Egypt. Eventually, Joseph's family was reunited in Egypt.

29 **Joseph (Jesus' earthly father)**—Husband of Mary and earthly father of Jesus. The carpenter Joseph was betrothed to Mary when she conceived Jesus.

He planned to divorce her quietly, but an angel told him not to fear marrying her, for she would bear the Messiah. With Mary, he traveled to Bethlehem, where the child was born. He was with Mary when Jesus was dedicated at the temple and when they visited the temple when Jesus was twelve years old.

30 **Joshua**—Moses' right-hand man. Joshua, the son of Nun, led Israel to victory against the Amalekites. He spied out Canaan before the Israelites entered it and came back with a positive report. For his faith, he was one of only two men of his generation who entered the Promised Land. God chose Joshua to succeed Moses as Israel's leader. After Moses' death, Joshua led the Israelites into the Promised Land.

31 **Judas Iscariot**—The disciple who betrayed Jesus, usually identified as Judas Iscariot. He was given his position by Jesus and was put in charge of the money, but he was not honest with it (John 12:6). Judas went to the chief priests and promised to betray Jesus for forty pieces of silver. At the Last Supper, Jesus predicted Judas' betrayal and even handed him a morsel of food to indicate his identity as the betrayer. Sorrowful at his betrayal, following Jesus' death, Judas returned the money to the priests and hanged himself.

32 **Luke**—Known as the "beloved physician," Luke was probably a Gentile believer who became a companion of Paul. Writer of a gospel and the book of Acts, he was also an excellent historian, as is shown by the exactness with which he describes the details of the gospel events and the places where they happened.

The use of "we" in Acts 16:10 indicates that Luke joined Paul and Silas on their missionary journey. He was with Paul during his imprisonment in Rome.

33 **Mary**—Jesus' mother, who as a virgin received the news from an angel that she would bear the Messiah. Mary traveled with her betrothed, Joseph, to Bethlehem, where Jesus was born. When she and Joseph brought Jesus to the temple, Mary heard Simeon and Anna's prophecies about her son. When Jesus was twelve years old, the couple brought Him to the temple, did not realize He had not left with their group, and had to return for Him. Mary stood by the cross as Jesus was crucified and was in the upper room with the disciples after His ascension.

34 **Matthew**—A tax collector (or publican), also called Levi, who left his tax booth to follow Jesus. Disciple Matthew was in the upper room, following Jesus' resurrection, praying. Although Matthew does not list himself as writer of the gospel named after him, the early church ascribed it to him.

35 **Moses**—The Old Testament prophet through whom God gave Israel the law. Because Pharaoh commanded that all male newborn Israelites should be killed, Moses' mother placed him in a basket in the Nile River. There he was found by an Egyptian princess, who raised him. Grown, Moses killed a man for abusing an Israelite slave and fled to Midian, where he met God in a burning bush. The Lord sent Moses back to Egypt, where his brother Aaron became his spokesman. As God's prophet in Egypt,

Moses confronted Pharaoh, telling him to let God's people go.

36 **Nebuchadnezzar**—Twice this king of Babylon besieged Jerusalem, took its king, and brought Judah's people into exile. King Jehoiakim of Judah had been Nebuchadnezzar's vassal for three years when he rebelled. Nebuchadnezzar attacked Jerusalem and took him, his family, with his servants, princes, and officers. He left only the poorest people in the nation's capital. Babylon's king also took the palace and temple treasures. Zedekiah, made king by Nebuchadnezzar, also rebelled. When his city was starving, the king and his soldiers fled. Nebuchadnezzar pursued, captured Zedekiah, killed his sons, put out his eyes, and carried him to Babylon.

37 **Nehemiah**—Sent at his own request, by Persian King Artaxerxes, to rebuild Jerusalem, Nehemiah became the governor of Jerusalem. Under his rule, Jerusalem's walls were rebuilt.

38 **Nicodemus**—A member of the Jewish Sanhedrin who came to Jesus by night to question Him about His miracles. Jesus told Nicodemus he had to be born again. When the Pharisees wanted to arrest Jesus, Nicodemus stood up for Him. He provided the spices with which Jesus' body was wrapped after His death.

39 **Noah**—The man God chose to build an ark that would save both animals and people. God gave Noah specific building directions. When his boat-building project was finished, he and his family entered the ark and God brought in seven of every clean animal

and two of the unclean. God caused it to rain for forty days and nights, until the world was flooded and everything else on earth was destroyed. For one hundred and fifty days, the ark floated, until the waters abated and the vessel rested on the mountains of Ararat.

40 **Paul**—God's chosen apostle to the Gentiles. Paul zealously persecuted Christians until he became one himself as he traveled to Damascus and was confronted by Jesus. Scripture begins calling him Paul when he and Barnabas set out on the first of Paul's three missionary journeys. He communicated with the churches and with individuals through his epistles, or letters. He wrote to the Romans, Corinthians, Ephesians, Galatians, Philippians, Colossians, Thessalonians, and also wrote letters to Titus, Timothy, and Philemon. These form part of his contribution to the New Testament.

41 **Peter**—Jesus' disciple, also called Simon Peter and Simon Bar-Jonah, who was called from his fishing, along with his brother Andrew, to become a fisher of men. The brothers were among Jesus' most intimate disciples. Following the giving of the Great Commission, Peter spoke out boldly in his Pentecost sermon. He healed the lame beggar at the temple gate and refused to stop preaching when the Jewish Council arrested him. He had a vision about the acceptance of Gentile believers in the church but later failed to support them. He wrote the books of 1 and 2 Peter.

42 **Ruth**—A Moabite woman, Ruth married Naomi's son Mahlon while the family lived in Moab during a famine. When Ruth's husband, his brother, and his father died, Ruth's mother-in-law decided to move back to Bethlehem. Though her sister-in-law, Orpah, went back to her own family, Ruth refused to leave Naomi. Together they went to Bethlehem, and there Ruth gleaned the barley harvest to provide food for them. Boaz became aware of Ruth and became kinsman-redeemer for her and Naomi. Ruth married Boaz and had a son Obed, who was considered Naomi's grandson.

43 **Samson**—Twelfth judge of Israel. He was called to follow a Nazarite vow, which meant he could not eat or drink anything from a grapevine, drink alcohol, cut his hair, or eat anything unclean. Samson performed amazing feats of strength. When he married, Samson chose a Philistine woman. God used the union to confront the Philistines, who ruled over Israel. Betrayed by his wife, Samson took out his anger on her people, burning their grain and performing more feats of strength. He fell in love with the Philistine woman Delilah, which led to his ultimate downfall.

44 **Samuel**—Prophet and judge of Israel. After Samuel was weaned, his mother brought him to Eli the priest to live at the temple and serve the Lord. Eli realized that God had spoken to Samuel and encouraged the boy to listen and respond. In his first prophecy, Samuel spoke out against the wickedness of Eli's sons.

Samuel led the Israelites to repent of their idolatry, and he judged Israel for his whole life.

45 **Sarah**—The name God gave Sarai, wife of Abram (Abraham), after He promised she would bear a child. Though she was ninety years old, God repeated the promise to give Abraham a son by her. When Sarah heard this, she laughed. A year later she bore Isaac. When Abraham's son Ishmael—child of Sarah's maid, Hagar—mocked Isaac, Sarah feared for her own son and had Hagar and Ishmael sent out of Abraham's camp. When Sarah died, Abraham bought land from the Hittites and buried her in the cave of Machpelah.

46 **Saul**—The first monarch of the nation of Israel. Anointed king of Israel by the prophet Samuel, Saul fought the Philistines throughout his reign. But after the king wrongly made a burnt offering to God at Michmash, Samuel told Saul that because of his sin, his kingdom would not be established forever, and God would seek a man after his own heart. When God ordered Saul to fight the Amalekites and kill all the people and cattle, Saul did not kill their king or cattle. God rejected him as Israel's king, and Samuel anointed David king.

47 **Silas**—A prophet chosen by the Jerusalem Council to accompany Paul and Barnabas to the Gentiles. After Barnabas and Paul separated, Paul took Silas on a new journey. Together they were imprisoned in Philippi after Paul freed a slave girl of an evil spirit. They led the jailer and his family to Christ and continued their mission in Greece.

48 **Solomon**—Son of King David and Bathsheba, Solomon was loved by God. Despite the efforts of his half brother Adonijah to take the throne, Solomon became king over Israel with the support of his father, David. When God came to Solomon in a vision and asked what he wanted, the king requested "an understanding heart" to rule His people (1 Kings 3:9). Because Solomon asked wisely, God gave him wisdom, understanding, and the wealth and honor he had not requested. Solomon built the Lord's temple with the aid of Hiram, Tyre's king. Solomon dedicated the temple with a prayer and benediction.

49 **Stephen**—A man of the Jewish church, "full of faith and of the Holy Ghost" (Acts 6:5), Stephen was ordained to care for the physical needs of church members. He became involved in a disagreement with Jews who accused him of blasphemy. After witnessing to the Jewish council, Stephen was stoned by an angry mob that included Saul, later called the apostle Paul.

50 **Timothy**—Coworker of the apostle Paul, his name is joined with Paul's in the introductory greetings in 2 Corinthians, Philippians, Colossians, and Philemon. Paul also wrote two epistles of guidance to this young pastor who was like a son to him.

IMPORTANT BIBLICAL LEADERS

Throughout biblical history, God appointed men and women as political and religious leaders of their people. Some of those leaders served God faithfully, but many did not. Here are some of those important leaders and the office they held:

THE TWELVE SPIES OF CANAAN
(NUMBERS 13:4–15)

1. From the tribe of Reuben, Shammua the son of Zaccur.

2. From the tribe of Simeon, Shaphat the son of Hori.

3. From the tribe of Judah, Caleb the son of Jephunneh.

4. From the tribe of Issachar, Igal the son of Joseph.

5. From the tribe of Ephraim, Oshea [Joshua] the son of Nun.

6. From the tribe of Benjamin, Palti the son of Raphu.

7. From the tribe of Zebulun, Gaddiel the son of Sodi.

8. From the tribe of Joseph, namely, of the tribe of Manasseh, Gaddi the son of Susi.

9. From the tribe of Dan, Ammiel the son of Gemalli.

10. From the tribe of Asher, Sethur the son of Michael.

11. From the tribe of Naphtali, Nahbi the son of Vophsi.

12. From the tribe of Gad, Geuel the son of Machi.

THE JUDGES OF ISRAEL

1. **Othniel (Judges 3:7–11)**—Caleb's brother, who by capturing Kirjathsepher won the hand of Caleb's daughter, Achsah, in marriage. Othniel delivered

Israel from the king of Mesopotamia and judged Israel for forty years.

2. **Ehud (Judges 3:12–30)**—The second judge of Israel who subdued the oppressing Moabites. A left-handed man, Ehud killed Eglon, the obese king of Moab, with a hidden dagger while pretending to be on a peace mission.

3. **Shamgar (Judges 3:31)**—Fought bravely against the Philistines; killed 600 Philistine soldiers with an ox goad.

4. **Deborah (Judges 4–5)**—Israel's only female judge and prophetess, she held court under a palm tree. Deborah called Barak to lead warriors into battle against the Canaanite army commander, Sisera. But Barak would fight only if Deborah went with him. For this, she prophesied that God would hand Sisera over to a woman. Deborah supported Barak as he gathered his troops on Mount Tabor and advised him to go into battle. With him, she sang a song of victory that praised the Lord.

5. **Gideon (Judges 6–8)**—See Page 53

6. **Abimelech (Judges 9)**—A son of Gideon, by his concubine. He killed all but one of his brothers and was made king of Shechem. But three years later the Shechemites rebelled, and he destroyed the city. He moved on to attack Thebez, and there he was killed when a woman dropped part of a millstone on his head.

7. **Tola (Judges 10:1–2)**—Judged Israel for twenty-three years.

8. **Jair (10:3–5)**—The eighth judge of Israel, who led the nation for twenty-two years. He was known for having thirty sons who rode thirty donkeys.

9. **Jephthah (Judges 10:6–12:7)**—Eighth judge of Israel, Jephthah the Gileadite was Gilead's son by a prostitute. His half brothers drove him out, and he went to the land of Tob. When the Ammonites fought Israel, he became Gilead's leader. He unsuccessfully tried to make peace with these enemies. Then Jephthah promised God that he would sacrifice to Him whatever greeted him when he came home victorious. His daughter, his only child, came to greet him on his victorious return. After giving his daughter a two-month reprieve, Jephthan kept his vow. For passing over Ephraim's land, he battled the Ephraimites. Jephthah judged Israel for six years.

10. **Ibzan (Judges 12:8–10)**—The tenth judge of Israel, who led the nation for seven years. He was known for having thirty sons and thirty daughters. Ibzan sent his daughters abroad and brought in thirty foreign women as wives for his sons.

11. **Elon (Judges 12:11–12)**—Judged Israel for ten years.

12. **Abdon (Judges 12:13–15)**—The twelfth judge of Israel who led the nation for eight years. He was known for having forty sons and thirty nephews who each rode a donkey.

13. **Samson (Judges 13–16)**—Twelfth judge of Israel, from the time of his conception he was supposed to follow a Nazarite vow, which meant he could

not eat or drink anything from a grapevine, drink alcohol, cut his hair, or eat anything unclean. Samson performed amazing feats of strength. When he married, Samson chose a Philistine woman. God used the union to confront the Philistines, who ruled over Israel. Betrayed by his wife, Samson took out his anger on her people, burning their grain and performing more feats of strength.

14. **Eli (1 Samuel 1–4:18)**—The high priest in Shiloh, where the ark of the covenant rested for a time. He rebuked Hannah for being drunk as she prayed for God to give her a child. When her son Samuel was born, she brought him to Eli and dedicated him to God. Samuel began to hear the Word of God, and Eli encouraged him to listen. Though his own sons were spiritual failures, Eli did much better with his foster son. Samuel went on to be a powerful prophet of the Lord.

15. **Samuel (1 Samuel 7:15)**—Samuel was born after his mother, Hannah, petitioned God to give her a child and promised to give him up to God's service in return. After Samuel was weaned, Hannah brought him to the priest Eli to live at the temple and serve the Lord. Eli realized that God had spoken to Samuel and encouraged the boy to listen and respond. In his first prophecy, Samuel spoke out against the wickedness of Eli's sons. Samuel led the Israelites to repent of their idolatry, and he judged Israel for his whole life.

KINGS OF ISRAEL/JUDAH

- **Saul (c. 1050–1010 BC)**—The first king of Israel; his reign began well but ended very badly.

- **David (c. 1010–969 BC)**—David ruled first over Judah and then over both Judah and Israel. Samuel anointed David king of Israel around 1023 BC.

- **Solomon (c. 970–930 BC)**—The son of David and Bathsheba, he reigned over the united kingdoms of Judah and Israel.

- **Rehoboam (c. 930 BC)**—The son of Solomon; the Kingdom of Israel was divided during his reign.

KINGS (AND ONE QUEEN) OF JUDAH:

1. **Rehoboam (c. 930–913 BC)—Mostly bad.** Son of King Solomon, Rehoboam inherited the kingdom of Israel. But his proud attitude toward his subjects' request for lower taxes made Israel rebel against him and set up Jeroboam as their king. Only the southern kingdom of Judah remained under Rehoboam's rule. The priests and Levites sided with Rehoboam because Jeroboam had set up idols in his nation and rejected God's spiritual leaders. But once Rehoboam had established his power, "he forsook the law of the LORD, and all Israel with him" (2 Chronicles 12:1).

2. **Abijah (c. 913–910 BC)—Mostly bad.** A son of King Rehoboam. He inherited the throne from his father and went to war against Jeroboam of Israel, claiming

that God had given Israel to David and his heirs.
Triumphant because his troops called on the Lord
in desperation, he gained some cities from Israel and
"waxed mighty" (2 Chronicles 13:21).

3. **Asa (c. 910–872 BC)—Good.** Son of King Abijam.
Asa reigned forty-one years and removed many idols
from Judah. While the country was peaceful, he
built fortified cities and established his army. When
an Ethiopian army attacked, he called on the Lord
and was victorious. When Azariah prophetically
encouraged the king to seek the Lord, Asa led his
people in making a covenant to seek God. He even
removed his mother from her position as queen
because she worshiped idols. But he did not remove
the idols from the high places.

4. **Jehoshaphat (c. 872–853 BC)—Good.** He inherited
the throne from his father, Asa. Though he had
blessings and "riches and honour in abundance" (2
Chronicles 17:5). he repeatedly allied himself with
Israel. Though he followed God, Jehoshaphat became
inconsistent in his obedience and did not completely
end idolatry in Judah. Despite the warning of the
prophet Micaiah, he joined King Ahab of Israel in a
disastrous attack on Ramoth-gilead. Later, as a great
army came against his own nation, Jehoshaphat
sought the Lord. When King Jehoram of Israel asked
Jehoshaphat to join him in attacking Moab, Judah's
king suggested they consult a prophet.

5. **Jehoram (c. 853–841 BC)—Bad.** Firstborn son of
King Jehoshaphat. After Jehoram became king, he

killed all his brothers. He married the daughter of King Ahab of Israel and led his nation into idolatry. Philistines and Arabians invaded Judah and captured Jehoram's family. As God had warned, Jehoram died, unmourned, of an incurable bowel disease. He was not buried in the kings' tombs.

6. **Ahaziah (c. 841 BC)—Bad.** Son of Johoram and Athaliah. Following the advice of bad counselors, he joined with Joram, king of Israel, to fight against the Syrians. When Joram was wounded, Israel's king went to Jezreel, where the king of Judah visited him. There Jehu killed Joram and sent his men on to Samaria, after Ahaziah. Ahaziah died of his wounds in Megiddo.

7. **Queen Athaliah (c. 841–835 BC)—Very bad.** Wife of Jehoram and mother of Ahaziah, kings of Judah. When her son was killed by Jehu, she destroyed all possible heirs to the throne, missing only Joash, who was saved by his aunt Jehosheba. Wicked, idolatrous Athaliah ruled Judah for six years. In the seventh year of her reign, in the temple, the priest Jehoiada crowned Joash king. When Athaliah saw this, she declared it treason. Jehoiada commanded his warriors to take her outside the temple and kill her. Judah did not mourn her death.

8. **Joash (c. 835–796 BC)—Mostly good.** Son of King Ahaziah. He was hidden from his wicked grandmother Athaliah and protected by the priest Jehoiada, who instructed him. Though he followed the Lord, Joash did not remove idolatry from the nation. He ordered that money be collected to

refurbish the temple. But when Hazael, king of Syria, was about to attack, Joash took the gold from the temple and his own house and sent it as tribute to Hazael. Joash was killed by his servants, who formed a conspiracy against him.

9. **Amaziah (c. 796–792 BC) Mostly good.** Son and successor of King Joash. Though he did right, the new king did not remove the pagan altars from the land. He killed the servants who had murdered his father in his bed but did not kill their children. After raising an army in his country, he hired 100,000 men from Israel. But a man of God convinced the king to rely on God, not a hired army, so Amaziah sent the Israelites home. With his own men, he went to war with Edom and won; meanwhile the scorned Israelite army attacked Judah, killed 3,000, and carried away spoils.

10. **Uzziah, aka Azariah (c. 792–750 BC)—Mostly good.** Son of Amaziah. Uzziah obeyed God, and the Lord helped him fight the Philistines and other enemies. The king fortified Jerusalem and built a powerful army. But in his power, Uzziah became proud and wrongly burned incense on the temple's incense altar. Confronted by the priests, he became angry. God immediately made him a leper. Thereafter Uzziah was cut off from the temple, and his son Jotham ruled in his name.

11. **Jotham (c. 750–735 BC)—Good.** Son of Uzziah, Jotham governed for his father, who had become a leper. After he inherited the throne, he built the upper gate of the temple and obeyed God, but he did

not destroy the idolatry in the land. He defeated the Ammonites and received tribute from them.

12. **Ahaz (c. 735–715 BC)—Wicked.** He became deeply involved in paganism. God sent the kings of Syria and Israel against Judah in punishment, and Ahaz was unsuccessful in fighting off his enemies. Many people of Judah were carried off. Ahaz sent to Tiglath-pileser, king of Assyria, for help, offering gifts to the pagan king. The Assyrian army responded by attacking Damascus. When Ahaz joined the Assyrian king in Damascus, he saw and admired a pagan altar and had it copied. When he returned to Jerusalem, he commanded Urijah the priest to use this pagan altar for worship.

13. **Hezekiah (c. 715–697 BC)—Very good.** See page 54

14. **Manasseh (c. 697–642 BC)—Very bad, but with a good end.** The son of Hezekiah, Manasseh erected pagan altars in the temple and led his nation into idolatry. He burned his own sons as offerings to the idols and became involved in witchcraft. The Lord caused the Assyrian army to capture Manasseh and bring him to Babylon. Manasseh repented, and God brought him back to Jerusalem. He removed the idols from Jerusalem, repaired God's altar, and commanded his nation to follow God.

15. **Amon (c. 642–640 BC)—Very bad.** An evil king who reigned two years. He worshiped idols and "trespassed more and more" (2 Chronicles 33:23). His servants conspired against him and killed him in his own house.

16. **Josiah (c. 640–609 BC)—Very Good.** The son of King Amon, Josiah became king when he was eight years old and followed the Lord closely through his life. Josiah collected money and repaired the temple. When the book of the law was discovered by Hilkiah the priest, Josiah had it read to him and consulted the prophetess Huldah. Then Josiah read the book to the elders of his nation, made a covenant to follow the Lord, and caused his people to follow his example. He put down idolatry in the land and celebrated the Passover.

17. **Jehoahaz (c. 609 BC)—Bad. Son of King Josiah.** This evil king reigned only three months before Pharaoh Necho of Egypt captured Jehoahaz and sent him to Egypt, where he died.

18. **Jehoiakim (c. 609–598 BC)—Very bad.** Originally named Eliakim, he was a son of King Josiah. After the Egyptian Pharaoh Necho killed Josiah and later deposed his son Jehoahaz, the pharaoh made Eliakim king of Judah and changed his name to Jehoiakim. Following Necho's defeat by King Nebuchadnezzar, Jehoiakim served the Babylonian king. But three years later, Jehoiakim rebelled. When Jeremiah's prophetic, warning words were read to this wicked king, he burned the scroll they were written on. So God declared that Babylon would destroy Judah. Nebuchadnezzar attacked Jerusalem, bound Jehoiakim in chains, and carried him to Babylon.

19. **Jehoiachin (c. 598–597 BC)—Bad.** The son of King Jehoiakim, this evil king reigned only three months before King Nebuchadnezzar of Babylon carried him

and the best of his people to Babylon. In the thirty-seventh year of Jehoiachin's captivity, King Evil-Merodach brought him out of prison and gave him preferential treatment.

20. **Zedekiah (c. 597–586 BC)—Bad.** Originally named Mattaniah, Zedekiah was a brother of King Jehoiachin. Nebuchadnezzar conquered Judah, deposed Jehoiachin, renamed Mattaniah Zedekiah, and made him king. Like his brother, Zedekiah rebelled against Babylon. Zedekiah did not heed the prophet Jeremiah and imprisoned him. Nebuchadnezzar besieged Jerusalem. When the city no longer had food, Zedekiah and his troops sought to escape. The Chaldean army caught Zedekiah, killed his sons before him, and put out his eyes. They bound him and carried him to Babylon.

KINGS OF ISRAEL (NORTHERN KINGDOM):

1. **Jeroboam I (c. 930–909 BC)—Bad.** A servant of King Solomon who had authority over the forced labor for the tribes of Ephraim and Manasseh. The prophet Ahijah the Shilonite prophesied that Jeroboam would be king over ten tribes of Israel when Solomon died. Solomon heard this and sought to kill Jeroboam, who fled to Egypt. Israel rebelled against Solomon's son, King Rehoboam, and made Jeroboam king. Fearing his people would return to Rehoboam if they worshiped in Jerusalem, Jeroboam established idolatrous worship in Israel.

2. **Nadab (c. 909–908 BC)—Bad.** Son of Jeroboam who inherited his throne. Nadab did evil and made his country sin. Baasha conspired against Nadab and killed him at Gibbethon, then usurped his throne.

3. **Baasha (c. 908–886 BC)—Bad.** The idolatrous king who fought with Asa, king of Judah. After conspiring against and killing Nadab, he took Israel's throne. Baasha attempted to fortify Ramah, to limit access to Judah. But Asa bribed Ben-hadad, king of Syria, who had a covenant with both nations, to support him instead of Baasha. Asa's army tore down the unfinished fortifications at Ramah and carried the stones away. Baasha and Asa fought for the rest of their reigns. Jehu, son of Hanani, prophesied the destruction of Baasha's household. This occurred when Baasha's son, Elah, was killed by Zimri.

4. **Elah (c. 886–885 BC)—Bad.** A contemporary of Asa, king of Judah, Elah was killed by Zimri, who usurped his throne.

5. **Zimri (c. 885 BC)—Bad.** After usurping Elah's throne, Zimri killed Elah's male relatives, fulfilling the prophecy of Jehu. Zimri reigned seven days before Israel made Omri king in his place. When the capital was taken, Zimri burned down the king's house with himself inside it.

6. **Tibni (c. 885–880 BC)—Bad.** The losing contender for the throne of Israel after Zimri killed King Elah.

7. **Omri (c. 885–874 BC)—Very bad.** Commander of Israel's army under King Elah. After Zimri killed

Elah, the people made Omri king. Omri and his army besieged Zimri at Tirzah and took the city. Omri overcame those who supported Tibni for king. Omri did evil and made Israel sin.

8. **Ahab (c. 874–853 BC)—Among the worst.** Ahab did great evil. He married Jezebel, daughter of the king of Zidon, and fell into Baal worship. God sent Israel a drought that only the prophet Elijah could break. Ahab coveted the vineyard of Naboth, who refused to sell his inheritance to him. While the king sulked, Jezebel plotted to kill Naboth and get the land. Because Ahab humbled himself before God, the Lord promised to bring evil in his son's life instead of visiting it on Ahab. He was killed in a battle with Syria.

9. **Ahaziah (c. 853–852 BC)—Bad.** The son of Ahab, he reigned for two years and walked in the pagan ways of his parents. When he fell through a lattice in his chamber and was badly hurt, he sought help from the pagan god Baalzebub. God sent Elijah to the king's messenger, asking if there was no God in Israel. Twice Ahaziah sent soldiers to Elijah, to demand that he come to the king. Twice Elijah called fire down upon them. When a third captain came more humbly, Elijah went to the king and prophesied that he would die.

10. **Joram (c. 852–841 BC)—Mostly bad.** Son of King Ahab. When he went to war with King Ahaziah of Judah against the Syrians, Joram was wounded. While he was recovering in Jezreel, he was killed by Jehu, who took his throne. Same as Jehoram.

11. **Jehu (c. 841–814 BC)—Mostly bad.** God commanded

Elijah to anoint Jehu king to destroy King Ahab and his dynasty. Jehu received Elijah's servant and the anointing. Jehu killed kings Joram of Israel and Ahaziah of Judah. Then he killed Jezebel, made the Samaritans slaughter Ahab's sons, and killed forty-two of King Ahaziah's relatives. After calling the priests of Baal and the idol's worshipers together, Jehu had his men put them all to the sword. But Jehu did not walk carefully in God's ways and lost part of Israel to Syria.

12. **Jehoahaz (c. 814–798 BC)—Bad.** The son of King Jehu, Jehoahaz did what was evil in God's sight. He fought and lost battles with Hazael, king of Syria. When he sought the Lord concerning the oppression that the nation inflicted upon Israel, God provided a savior.

13. **Jehoash (c. 798–793 BC)—Bad.** An evil king, son of King Jehoahaz. Jehoash regained from Hazael, king of Syria, the cities Hazael had won from Israel in battle. Jehoash fought King Amaziah of Judah, broke down Jerusalem's wall, and took gold and silver from the temple and the king. With hostages, he returned to Samaria.

14. **Jeroboam II (c. 793–753 BC)—Bad.** The son of King Joash, Jeroboam continued the idolatrous worship established by Jeroboam I. God used Jeroboam to regain Israel's lost territory, and he even took the Syrian capital, Damascus. The prophet Amos predicted Jeroboam's death by the sword.

15. **Zachariah (c. 753–752 BC)—Bad.** Son of King Jeroboam, Zachariah reigned over Israel for six months before he was killed by the conspirator Shallum.

16. **Shallum (c. 752 BC)—Bad.** The fifth-to-last king of the northern kingdom of Israel. Shallum obtained the throne by assassinating King Zachariah. Shallum was himself assassinated only one month later.

17. **Menahem (c. 752–742 BC)—Bad.** A king who usurped the throne from King Shallum. During his ten-year reign, the idolatrous Menahem did evil. To keep his throne, he raised money from the wealthy men of Israel and gave it to Pul, king of Assyria, as tribute.

18. **Pekahiah (c. 742–740 BC)—Bad.** Evil ruler who succeeded his father Menahem as king. Pekah conspired against Menahem and usurped his throne.

19. **Pekah (c. 752–732 BC)—Bad.** Captain of King Pekahiah of Israel, Pekah conspired against his king, killed him, and usurped his throne. Pekah was an evil king. The Assyrian king Tigleth-Pileser conquered portions of Israel during Pekah's reign.

20. **Hoshea (c. 732–722 BC)—Bad.** The Israelite who conspired against King Pekah, killed him, and took his throne. He became vassal to King Shalmaneser of Assyria, but sent messengers to the king of Egypt. Shalmaneser imprisoned Hoshea, captured Samaria, and carried the Israelites off to Assyria.

WHERE IT ALL HAPPENED: IMPORTANT PLACES IN THE BIBLE

50 OF THE MOST IMPORTANT PLACES IN THE BIBLE

1. **Ai**—A city east of Bethel that Joshua's spies reported did not have many inhabitants. Joshua sent three thousand men to conquer the city, but his soldiers fled before its warriors. When Joshua prayed about the defeat, God told him Israel had sinned. Once Joshua identified the sinner, Achan, and had him stoned, God commanded the Israelites to again attack the city, which He would give into their hands (see Joshua 7–8).

2. **Antioch**—The capital of Syria. The church in Jerusalem sent Barnabas to Antioch, when they heard that Gentiles were hearing the Word. Cypriot Jews who had heard the message had shared it with Greeks. Barnabas went to Tarsus, to get Saul's assistance in his mission. In this city, believers first received the name *Christians*. Paul and Barnabas received their missionary calling in Antioch (see Acts 11:19–26).

3. **Armageddon**—A symbolic name for the place where the apostle John foretold there will be the last, great battle on earth, fought between the antichrist and Jesus (see Revelation 16:16).

4. **Asia**—A Roman province in the western part of Asia

Minor, whose capital was Ephesus. For a time, the Holy Spirit prohibited Paul from preaching in Asia (Acts 16:6–8), but Paul came to Ephesus on his second missionary journey and remained there two years, spreading the gospel to the whole province. When Demetrius the silversmith started a riot over Paul's preaching, the apostle moved on to Macedonia (Acts 19). Peter wrote his first epistle in part to the believers of Asia, and John addressed his Revelation to "the seven churches which are in Asia" (Revelation 1:4).

5. **Assyria**—An empire that spread from its original nation in the upper plain of Mesopotamia to incorporate a wide arc of land that swept from Egypt, north through Syria and Palestine to eastern Asia Minor, and west to Babylonia and the Persian Gulf. During the reign of Hezekiah's son, Manasseh, Assyria attacked Judah, captured the king, and carried him and many of his people to Babylon (2 Chronicles 33:11). When Manasseh humbled himself before God, he was returned to his position in Jerusalem. God promised that Assyria would be punished and a remnant of Judah would return to the Lord (Isaiah 10:12, 21).

6. **Athens**—An influential Greek city on the peninsula of Attica, Athens was famed for its culture and philosophy. Paul traveled there from Berea, after the Jews of Thessalonica had stirred up trouble for him. Distressed by Athens' idolatry, which he would have seen at every turn at the Acropolis which held many temples, the apostle preached the gospel in the synagogue. Then at the invitation of the Athenian

philosophers, he spoke at Mars' hill (the Areopagus), to them and the members of the council of the Areopagus (see Acts 17:15–34).

7. **Babylon**—An ancient Mesopotamian city on the Euphrates River. Babylon's location made it an important city of trade. Genesis 10:8–10 describes Babel (some versions translate this "Babylon") as the start of Nimrod's kingdom. During the Old Babylonian Empire and King Hammurabi, the city reached a peak it would not match until the Neo-Babylonian Empire. The Kassite Nebuchanezzar I made it his capital. Under the Assyrians, Babylon was destroyed by Sennacherib, then rebuilt by Ashurbanipal. In the New Testament, Peter refers to a church at Babylon. In the book of Revelation, Babylon takes on a symbolic meaning as a fallen, sinful city.

8. **Bethany**—A village about two miles outside of Jerusalem. Bethany is best known as the home of Jesus' friends Lazarus, Martha, and Mary. When Lazarus became ill, Jesus did not come to the village until after Lazarus had died. When He did arrive, Martha and Mary mourned that He had not been there to prevent their brother's death. Jesus brought his friend back to life, causing trouble with the chief priests, who wanted to kill Him (John 11). Mary of Bethany anointed Jesus with oil prior to His crucifixion (John 12:1–3).

9. **Bethlehem**—Also called Bethlehem in Judea, to identify it from another Bethlehem northwest of Nazareth, this town south of Jerusalem was the

birthplace of Jesus, as foretold by the prophet Micah, who called it Bethlehem Ephratah. The wise men visited the young Jesus here and offered Him gifts of gold, frankincense, and myrrh. God warned them in a dream not to report back to Herod, who had told them where to find the child. Then God warned Joseph to take his family into Egypt, to avoid Herod's anger (Matthew 2:1–14).

10. **Caesarea**—Known as Caesarea Philippi, to differentiate it from the Caesarea built by Herod the Great. Here Jesus asked His disciples, "Whom do men say that I am?" Then He asked them whom they said He was. Peter answered, "Thou art the Christ" (Mark 8:27–29).

11. **Cana**—A Galilean village where Jesus and His disciples attended a wedding and the Lord performed His first miracle, turning water into wine. The family who was holding the wedding ran out of wine, so Mary, Jesus' mother, came to Him with the news. He told the servants to fill six large water jars with twenty to thirty gallons of water. When they drew the liquid out again, it was a good wine (John 2:1–11). Jesus' disciple Nathanael also came from Cana.

12. **Canaan**—The land east of the Mediterranean Sea as far as the Jordan River, and from the Taurus Mountains, going south beyond Gaza. Canaan included the areas later called Phoenicia, Palestine, and Syria. Its inhabitants were the descendants of Noah's grandson Canaan, including his firstborn child, Sidon, the Hittites, Jebusites, Amorites,

Girgasites, Hivites, Arkites, Sinites, Arvadites,
Zemarites, and Hamathites (Genesis 10:15–18).
God brought Abram and his family from Ur of the
Chaldees to Canaan. Promising they would become a
great nation there, the Lord promised Abram that his
descendants would own the land and that He would
be their God.

13. **Capernaum**—Jesus chose Capernaum, a village
    on the Sea of Galilee's north shore, as His ministry
    headquarters. He left Nazareth for Capernaum when
    Herod imprisoned John the Baptist. Thus He fulfilled
    the prophecy of Isaiah that Zebulun (which was the
    tribe of Nazareth) and Naphtali (which was the tribe
    of Capernaum) would see a great light. Jesus taught in
    Capernaum's synagogue. From here, He called several
    disciples—fishermen Peter, Andrew, James, and John,
    and the tax collector Matthew. He performed many
    miracles here as well.

14. **Colosse**—A city in the Roman province of Phrygia,
    in Asia Minor. The apostle Paul wrote the book of
    Colossians to the Christians in Colosse (Colossians
    1:2). He probably ministered in Colosse when he
    visited Phrygia.

15. **Corinth**—A Greek city, a trading center and capital
    of the Roman province of Achaia. Paul visited
    Corinth during his second missionary journey,
    after he ministered in Athens. In Corinth Paul met
    fellow tentmakers Aquila and Priscilla, who became
    friends and co-laborers with him. Paul preached
    in the Corinthian synagogue until the Jews there

strongly opposed him. Paul wrote two epistles (1 and 2 Corinthians) to the troubled church at Corinth. A letter of rebuke, written between the two letters that appear in scripture, seems to have been lost.

16. **Damascus**—An ancient Syrian city, northeast of Tyre, that King David conquered when the Syrians supported Hadadezer, king of Zobah, in battle. Following David's conquest, Damascus paid Israel tribute (2 Samuel 8:1–6). Near Damascus, the Pharisee Saul (later the apostle Paul) was confronted by Christ. Temporarily blinded, he had to be led into the city, where Ananias healed him. Converted, Saul quickly began preaching Christ in the synagogues of Damascus (Acts 9:3–20).

17. **Eden**—A garden God planted for Adam to live in, just after His creation. Eden was filled with pleasant trees and plants for food. God made the animals and had Adam name them. Adam and Eve were to care for Eden, but were commanded not to eat of "the tree of the knowledge of good and evil." When they listened to the serpent and disobeyed God's command, God sent the couple out of the garden, so they could not eat of the tree of life and live forever in their sin (Genesis 2–3).

18. **Edom**—The land of Esau (who was also called Edom), which was inhabited by his descendants and lay south of Moab and southeast of the Dead Sea, south of Zered Brook. The prophet Jeremiah describes the inhabitants of this mountainous nation as living "in the clefts of the rock, that holdest the height of

the hill" (Jeremiah 49:16). Edom was ruled by kings well before Israel established a kingly line. Refused permission to cross Edom on its King's Highway, Israel traveled just beyond the edge of that nation on their way to the Promised Land.

19. **Ephesus**—Capital of the Roman province of Asia, in the western part of Asia Minor. On his way to Jerusalem, Paul stopped in Ephesus and spoke to the Jews in its synagogue. Apollos preached in the city, only knowing the baptism of John the Baptist, but when Priscilla and Aquila heard his preaching, they taught him the full way of God (Acts 18:19–19:41). From prison in Rome, Paul wrote an epistle to the Ephesian church that focuses on the need for unity in the body of Christ.

20. **Galatia**—A Roman province in the center of Asia Minor. For a time, the Holy Spirit forbade Paul and Silas to preach here. But later, Paul strengthened the disciples in the provinces of Galatia and Phrygia. The apostle reminded the church of Galatia that he first preached to them because of an illness he suffered (Galatians 4:13). Paul wrote an epistle to the Galatians to establish the authority for his apostleship, to counter the influence of the Judaizers who had swayed some Galatians away from the gospel, and to encourage them to believe in salvation by grace.

21. **Galilee**—An area in the north of Israel that may originally have been in the inheritance of the tribe of Naphtali. Israel did not overpower the people who inhabited the area, so it became a racially mixed

area, earning it the name "Galilee of the Gentiles."
In Nazareth, a city of Galilee, Mary received the
news that she would bear the Messiah. Following
Jesus' birth and the family's flight into Egypt, Joseph
received an angelic message that he was to return
to Israel. He brought his family to Galilee to avoid
the rule of Archelaeus, a son of Herod the Great
(Matthew 2:13–23).

22. **Gethsemane**—A garden across the Kidron Valley
from Jerusalem, on the Mount of Olives. Jesus brought
His disciples to Gethsemane where He prayed, asking
the Father to take the cup of crucifixion from Him.
Despite His deep sorrow, Jesus accepted His Father's
will, while His nearby disciples, Peter, James, and John,
fell asleep. An armed crowd came to Gethsemane, and
Jesus was arrested following Judas's betrayal of Him
with a kiss. The disciples fled as their Master was led
away to face the Sanhedrin (Matthew 26:36–56).

23. **Golgotha**—The place near Jerusalem where Jesus was
crucified. Golgotha is mentioned by all the gospel
writers except Luke, who calls it by the Latin name,
Calvary. Scripture tells us Golgotha was beyond the
walls of the city: "Jesus also suffered outside the city
gate" (Hebrews 13:12 NIV). John adds that there was
a garden there, and an unused tomb in which He was
buried (John 19:41–42). Also known as Calvary.

24. **Jericho**—A Moabite city west of the Jordan River. The
Israelites entered Canaan, crossing the Jordan River
near Jericho, and camped in the Jericho plain as they
conquered the Midianites. God gave Joshua an unusual

battle plan to take Jericho: For six days Israel's soldiers were to walk once around the city; on the seventh day they were to go around the city seven times, with the priests walking before the troops, blowing their trumpets and carrying the ark of the covenant. When the priests made a long blast, the people were to shout, and Jericho would be theirs (Joshua 6).

25. **Jerusalem**—The city of Jerusalem played a huge part in biblical history. After King David passed his throne to his son Solomon, the new king built the temple in Jerusalem. Centuries later, as Jesus headed toward Jerusalem, just before His death, He recognized that His death had to take place in the city. At Pentecost, in Jerusalem, the Holy Spirit filled believers, and they spoke with other tongues. Here Stephen was martyred after he preached the gospel with power. Jerusalem remained important, even as the church spread beyond Israel.

26. **Joppa**—A Mediterranean seaport city in the territory of the tribe of Daniel Huram (or Hiram) of Tyre shipped cedar logs to King Solomon through Joppa, for his building projects in Jerusalem. When Israel rebuilt the temple, following the Babylonian Exile, they used the same route. To escape God's command to go to Nineveh, the prophet Jonah went to Joppa, seeking a ship bound for Tarshish (Jonah 1:3). At Simon the tanner's house, in Joppa, Peter saw a vision he understood as God's message that he should accept Gentiles who believed in Jesus (Acts 10:8–48).

27. **Jordan River**—A river flowing from Palestine's Lake

Huleh, south to the Sea of Galilee and on to the Dead Sea; the Jordan River defined the eastern edge of Canaan. On its way toward Canaan, Israel conquered lands east of the Jordan River, including the eastern part of the Amorite holdings. Following the conquest of the Promised Land, most of Israel's land lay west of the Jordan. John the Baptist performed many baptisms in the Jordan River, including the baptism of Jesus (Matthew 3:6, 13–17).

28. **Kadesh**—A place in the Desert of Zin from which Chedoralomer, king of Elam, and his allies attacked the Amalekites and Amorites. From Kadesh, Moses sent out the spies into the Promised Land (Numbers 13). After Israel refused to enter the Promised Land, Israel lived in a camp in Kadesh "many days" (Deuteronomy 1:46). Miriam died in Kadesh, and the rock of Meribah, which Moses disobediently struck two times, was near here (Numbers 20:14–17).

29. **Laodicea**—A city of the Roman province of Phrygia. Paul had not yet visited the church in Laodicea when he wrote the Colossians. Paul told the nearby church at Colosse that Epaphras, "a servant of Christ" (Colossians 4:12), had a great zeal for their congregation and the church at Laodicea. The epistle to the Colossians was written to be read in both churches. The apostle John delivered a message from Jesus to the church at Laodicea, stating that the believers there had grown lukewarm (Revelation 3:14–22).

30. **Lystra**—A Lycaonian city to which Paul and Barnabas fled after the Jews of Iconium tried to stone

them. In Lystra Paul healed a lame man. The people of the city responded by declaring Paul and Barnabas gods. But the Jews of Antioch and Iconium followed the apostles to Lystra and stoned Paul (Acts 14:6–20). Though they left Lystra, Paul and Barnabas returned later to encourage the believers there. The Christians of Lystra and Iconium gave a good report about Timothy, so Paul took him on his missionary travels.

31. **Midian**—A land east of the Sinai peninsula, in the northwest portion of Arabia. Midian lay east of the Gulf of Aqaba and south of Edom. Moses fled here after he killed an Egyptian (Exodus 2:11–15). He married Zipporah, daughter of the Midian priest Jethro. When Israel conquered the Promised Land, Midianites sought to lure Israel into idolatry and intermarriage. Cozbi, daughter of a Midianite prince, was killed when an Israelite brought her to his tent as Moses called Israel to turn away from foreign women.

32. **Moab**—At the time of the Israelites' return to the Promised Land, this nation, which was composed of the descendants of Lot and his eldest daughter (Genesis 19:37), lay east of the Dead Sea and below the Arnon River. At God's command, when they headed for the Promised Land, Israel skirted Moab and went through the Amorites' territory. But Moab's king, Balak, feared the Israelites and asked the pagan prophet Balaam to curse them. When Balaam could not, he counseled Balak to lead Israel into idolatry (Numbers 31:16). Moab periodically took arms against God's people. It joined Sisera in his attack on Israel.

33. **Mount Carmel**—The place where Elijah confronted Ahab, king of Israel, and the priests of Baal and suggested that he and Baal's priests each prepare a sacrifice then call on their God or gods and see which one(s) responded to the sacrifice. While the priests of Baal received no response, Elijah's God consumed the sacrifice with fire (1 Kings 18:19–42). Isaiah prophesied that Carmel would "see the glory of the Lord" (Isaiah 35:2), and Amos predicted that when the Lord roars from Zion, "the top of Carmel shall wither" (Amos 1:2), and those who hide there, He will "take them out thence" (Amos 9:3).

34. **Mount Olivet (Mount of Olives)**—A mountain ridge east of Jerusalem. King David fled from his son Absalom, grieving as he ascended the Olivet ridge (2 Samuel 15:30). Luke describes it as "a Sabbath day's journey" outside the city (Acts 1:12). From here, also, Jesus ascended into heaven.

35. **Mount Sinai**—A mountain in the south-central part of the peninsula between Egypt and the Promised Land. God called Moses to Mount Sinai and told him to sanctify the people (Exodus 19). God called Moses up, alone, to receive the Law. Moses was gone for many days, and his people became impatient and pressured Aaron into building a calf-shaped idol (Exodus 32). Enraged at their unfaithfulness, Moses broke the first covenant tablets when he returned. After the idol was destroyed, God called Moses back to Mount Sinai to receive a new copy (Exodus 34:1–2).

36. **Nazareth**—In this village of Galilee, the virgin Mary

heard the news that she would bear the Messiah.
After the death of Herod the Great, Joseph brought
Mary and Jesus out of Egypt and back to live in
Nazareth, which was beyond the reach of Archelaus,
son of Herod the Great. Here Jesus announced the
beginning of His ministry and the fulfillment of the
promise of the Good News and liberty for God's
people. Furious, the people of His hometown tried to
kill Him (Luke 4:28–29).

37. **Nile**—The name "Nile River" doesn't appear in
the King James Bible, but newer Bible translations
mention the Nile River as the stream where Pharaoh's
daughter found the baby Moses floating in a basket
(Exodus 2:3–5) and as the site of the ten plagues
(Exodus 7:15, 20). In these passages, the King James
refers to it as "the river."

38. **Nineveh**—An ancient city built by Asshur that became
the capital of the Assyrian Empire. Nineveh was
located on the Tigris River's eastern bank. When the
Assyrian King Sennacherib attacked Jerusalem, God
killed his troops, so the frightened king returned to
Nineveh. God sent Jonah to preach repentance to this
large city, which took a journey of three days to cross.
Amazingly, Nineveh's king declared that everyone in
the city should repent, and the people repented, fasting
and putting on sackcloth. Therefore God did not
destroy the city as He had threatened to do (Jonah 3).

39. **Philadelphia**—A city where one of the seven
churches of Asia Minor to whom the apostle John
wrote in the book of Revelation was located. Jesus

commended and encouraged this church which had kept His word and avoided denying His name. As a result God would protect them from the trials that lay ahead. But the Lord also warned the church to hold onto what they already had, so they would not lose their crown (Revelation 3:7–13).

40. **Philippi**—A chief city of northeastern Macedonia that Paul and his fellow laborers visited to preach the gospel. Here Lydia became a convert, and a slave girl with a spirit of divination was healed. But the slave's owners dragged Paul and Silas before the magistrates, and the two men were imprisoned. Their jailer was converted before these prisoners were released by the magistrates. From this city, Paul wrote the books of 1 and 2 Corinthians. Paul wrote an epistle to the believers of Philippi while he was in Rome.

41. **Rephidim**—A campsite of the Israelites on their way to the Promised Land. There was no water to drink at Rephidim, so God moved Israel to the rock of Horeb. While Israel was at Rephidim, they were attacked by the Amalekites. Moses stood on the top of the hill, and as long as his arms were raised, Israel prevailed (Exodus 17:11–13). When he grew tired, Aaron and Hur stood beside him and held his hands up until Joshua won the battle. Moses built an altar here and called it Jehovah-nissi, "God is my banner."

42. **Rome**—This city was the center of the New Testament world and the capital of the Roman Empire. Though Rome's political influence dominated New Testament believers, the city of Rome is not frequently

mentioned in scripture. The Roman emperor Claudius commanded Jews to depart from Rome, so Aquila and his wife, Priscilla, moved to Corinth, where they met the apostle Paul. The apostle longed to visit Rome and wrote to the Christians there. From Rome, Paul wrote the epistles of Galatians, Ephesians, Philippians, Colossians, 2 Timothy, and Philemon.

43. **Samaria**—During the New Testament era, Samaria was the central Roman province of western Palestine. Knowing the Jew's hatred for the Samaritans' theological error, Jesus used the example of the Good Samaritan to teach spiritual truth to the Jews (Luke 10:30–37). On the border between Samaria and Galilee, He healed the ten leprous men, of whom only one gave thanks. At Sychar, He spoke to a Samaritan woman about living water and declared Himself as the Messiah (John 4:4–26).

44. **Sardis**—A city northeast of Ephesus, in Asia Minor's district of Lydia. It is only mentioned in Revelation, in the letter to the seven churches of Asia Minor. Though the church at Sardis had a reputation for being alive in Christ, Jesus said they were dead and needed to repent. Only a few believers there were not defiled (Revelation 3:1–6).

45. **Shechem**—A place in the land of Canaan where Jacob bought some land and built an altar called El-elohe-Israel (Genesis 33:18–20). At the oak tree near Shechem, the patriarch buried all the idols in his household, before he built the altar at Beth-el. Following Israel's conquest of the Promised Land,

Shechem became one of the six cities of refuge established for those who had committed accidental murder. It was given to the Levites by the tribe of Ephraim. At Shechem, Joshua gave his last address to the people of Israel, reminding them of their history and the faithfulness of God (Joshua 24).

46. **Shiloh**—A town in the territory of Ephraim where the Israelites assembled after the battles to conquer the Promised Land. They set up the tabernacle, and at its door Joshua cast lots to give land to the seven tribes that had yet to receive any. Here, too, the Levites received cities and their suburbs, as God had commanded (Numbers 35:2). The tabernacle, Israel's worship center, remained at Shiloh until the time of Samuel. When Hannah, mother of the prophet Samuel, asked the Lord for a child, she went to Shiloh to pray (1 Samuel 1:1–28).

47. **Sodom**—One of five Canaanite "cities of the plain" that may have been at the southern end of the Dead Sea. Abram's nephew, Lot, chose this land when Abram offered him whatever area he preferred. Though the men of Sodom "were wicked and sinners before the Lord," Lot pitched his tents near the city. When the king of Sodom fought the Edomite King Chedorlaomer and his Mesopotamian allies, Abram rescued Lot, his people, and his goods (Genesis 14). When Abram learned that God planned to destroy Sodom and the other plain cities, he bargained with Him. The Lord agreed that if ten righteous people could be found within Sodom's walls, He would not

destroy the city (Genesis 18:16–33). When Abram's part of the bargain could not be fulfilled, and Sodom's men wanted to have sex with the angels who warned Lot to leave the city, the Lord took Lot's family out of Sodom and destroyed it with fire and brimstone (Genesis 19:1–29).

48. **Thessalonica**—A Macedonian city where Paul preached in the synagogue. Though some people of the city believed, others accused Christians of believing in a king other than Caesar. The Christians of the city sent Paul and Silas away to Berea (Acts 17). Thessalonica was the hometown of Aristarchus, who sailed with Paul as he was on his way to Rome.

49. **Tyre**—A fortified Phoenician port and center of trade, Tyre had two harbors and consisted of both an island and a city on the mainland. King David and his son/ successor Solomon had a strong trade relationship with Tyre (1 Kings 5:1–12; 1 Chronicles 22:4). People in Tyre heard of the miracles of Jesus and came to follow Him. Because a huge crowd gathered around Him, Jesus preached to them from a boat. When Jesus traveled to Tyre and Sidon, a Syrophoenician woman insisted that He help her daughter, who had an unclean spirit. Commending her great faith, Jesus healed her daughter (Matthew 15:21–28).

50. **Zion**—Originally the name for a fortified mound on one of Jerusalem's southern hills, Zion, or Mount Zion, became the name for the temple mount, then the city of Jerusalem, and was even sometimes applied to the whole nation of Israel. It is often used in a

poetic sense that glorifies God and Israel's role in bringing about His purposes. Solomon brought the ark of the covenant to Zion, where it was placed in the temple on the place that tradition claims is Mount Moriah. The temple was dedicated with sacrifices and a prayer by King Solomon (2 Chronicles 5–6).

50 OLD TESTAMENT PROPHECIES OF THE MESSIAH, JESUS CHRIST

PROPHECY	REFERENCE	FULFILLMENT
• Born of a woman	Genesis 3:15	Luke 2:7
• A descendant of Abraham	Genesis 18:18	Matthew 1:1
• Born in Bethlehem	Micah 5:2	Matthew 2:1
• Born of a virgin	Isaiah 7:14	Matthew 1:18
• Came for all people groups	Genesis 18:17–18	Acts 3:24–26
• A light to the Gentiles	Isaiah 9:1–2	Luke 2:28–32
• Came to do God's will	Psalm 40:7–8	John 5:30
• Came to glorify God	Isaiah 49:3	Matthew 15:30–31
• A prophet	Deuteronomy 18:15–19	John 6:14

PROPHECY	REFERENCE	FULFILLMENT
• Preached the Good News	Isaiah 61:1–2	Luke 4:17–22
• Spoke by God's authority	Deuteronomy 18:15–19	John 12:48–50
• Declared He was Son of God	Psalm 2:7	Mark 15:39
• Spoke in parables	Isaiah 6:9–10	Matthew 13:13–15
• Ministered in Galilee	Isaiah 9:1–2	Matthew 4:12–17
• Had compassion for the poor	Isaiah 42:3	Matthew 11:4–5
• A humble man	Zechariah 9:9	Matthew 11:29
• Healed the blind	Isaiah 35:5	Mark 10:51–52
• Healed the deaf	Isaiah 35:5	Mark 7:32–35
• Healed the lame	Isaiah 35:6	Matthew 12:10–13
• Rejected by His own people	Isaiah 53:3	John 1:11
• Grieved over the Jews' unbelief	Isaiah 49:4	Luke 19:41–42
• Triumphal entry into Jerusalem	Zechariah 9:9	John 12:13–14

PROPHECY	REFERENCE	FULFILLMENT
• Entered Jerusalem on a donkey	Zechariah 9:9	Matthew 21:6–9
• Leaders conspired against Him	Psalm 2:2	Matthew 26:3–4
• Suffered willingly	Isaiah 53:11	John 12:27
• Gave up His life to save mankind	Isaiah 53:12	Luke 23:46
• Shed His blood for all	Isaiah 52:15	Revelation 1:5
• Betrayed by a friend	Psalm 41:9	Mark 14:10
• Betrayed for 30 pieces of silver	Zechariah 11:12–13	Matthew 26:14–15
• Falsely accused	Isaiah 53:7	Matthew 26:60–61
• Oppressed and afflicted	Isaiah 53:7	Matthew 26:62–63
• Mocked and insulted	Psalm 22:6–8	Matthew 27:39–40
• Suffered for others	Isaiah 53:4–5	Matthew 8:16–17
• His face beaten and spat upon	Isaiah 50:6	Matthew 26:67
• His back whipped	Isaiah 50:6	Mark 15:15

PROPHECY	REFERENCE	FULFILLMENT
• Crucified with sinners	Isaiah 53:12	Matthew 27:38
• Died a violent death	Zechariah 13:7	Matthew 27:35
• Hands and feet pierced	Psalm 22:16	John 20:27
• Given gall and vinegar	Psalm 69:21	John 19:29
• Prophetic words used to mock Him	Psalm 22:8	Matthew 27:43
• Lots cast for His clothes	Psalm 22:18	John 19:23–24
• Prayed for His tormenters	Psalm 109:4	Luke 23:34
• Forsaken by God	Psalm 22:1	Mark 15:34
• No bones broken at death	Psalm 34:20	John 19:33
• His side pierced	Zechariah 12:10	John 19:34
• Buried with the rich	Isaiah 53:9	Matthew 27:57–60
• Raised from the dead	Psalm 16:10	Matthew 28:9
• Ascended to heaven	Psalm 68:18	Luke 24:50–51

APPROXIMATE DATES IN THE LIFE OF JESUS

* **4 or 5 BC**—His Birth
* **4 or 5 BC**—Journey to Egypt with His Family
* **3 or 4 BC**—Return from Egypt
* **AD 8**—Boyhood Visit to the Temple
* **AD 26**—The Ministry of John the Baptist
* **AD 26**—Baptized by John the Baptist
* **AD 26**—First Year of His Ministry (Year of Inauguration)
* **AD 27**—Second Year of His Ministry (Year of Popularity)
* **AD 28**—Third Year of His Ministry (Year of Opposition)
* **AD 29 or 30**—Year of His Death

JESUS' ORIGINAL 12 APOSTLES

* Simon (Peter)
* Andrew
* James (son of Zebedee)
* John (James' brother)
* Philip
* Bartholomew
* Thomas

- Matthew
- James (son of Alphaeus)
- Thaddaeus (aka, Judas, son of James or Lebbaeus)
- Simon the Zealot (aka, Judas, son of James)
- Judas Iscariot

15 IMPORTANT PLACES JESUS VISITED

1. **Bethany**—A village about two miles outside of Jerusalem. This was the home of Jesus' close friends Lazarus, Martha, and Mary and the site of one of His most famous miracles: raising Lazarus from the dead (John 11). Six days before the Last Supper, Jesus returned to Bethany and went to dinner at the home of Simon the Leper, in Bethany. There Mary of Bethany anointed him with oil (John 12:1–8). After His triumphal entry into Jerusalem, He stayed at Bethany.

2. **Bethsaida**—A town on the northeast of the Sea of Galilee where Jesus healed a blind man. In a desert place belonging to the city, Jesus preached to a crowd, then fed a crowd of five thousand from the loaves and fish of a boy's lunch (Matthew 14:15–21). After feeding the people, Jesus sent His disciples on to Bethsaida, in a boat, then came to them on the water. Some scholars believe that Bethsaida may have been at the spot where the Jordan River flows into the Sea of Galilee, and portions of the town may have been on each side of the river.

3. **Cana**—A Galilean village where Jesus and His disciples attended a wedding and the Lord performed His first miracle, turning water into wine. The family who was holding the wedding ran out of wine, so Mary, Jesus' mother, came to Him with the news. He told the servants to fill six large water jars with twenty to thirty gallons of water. When they drew the liquid out again, it was a good wine (John 2:6–10).

4. **Capernaum**—A village on the Sea of Galilee's north shore, Capernaum was chosen by Jesus as His ministry headquarters. He left Nazareth for Capernaum when Herod imprisoned John the Baptist (Matthew 4:12–17). Jesus taught in Capernaum's synagogue. From here, He called several disciples—fishermen Peter, Andrew, James, and John, and the tax collector Matthew, and He performed many miracles.

5. **Decapolis**—A territory defined by a confederation of ten cities settled by the Greeks, Decapolis was largely southeast of the Sea of Galilee, with an area west of the Jordan River around Scythopolis (Beth-shan). People from this area were among the crowd that followed Jesus early in His ministry. Jesus healed a deaf and mute man there (Mark 7:32) and also miraculously fed 4,000 people (Mark 8:1–9).

6. **Egypt**—An often-powerful nation southwest of Israel, in the northeastern corner of Africa. Following the birth of Jesus, God commanded Joseph to take Mary and Jesus into Egypt to escape Herod the Great's rage. After Herod's death, God recalled the family back to Israel (Matthew 2:13–21).

7. **The region of the Gerasenes/Gaderenes**—The name
   Gadara never actually appears in scripture, only the
   name of its people. Here Jesus healed the man with
   a legion of unclean spirits who lived among the
   tombs. Despite this amazing miracle, the Gadarenes
   requested that Jesus and His disciples leave their land
   (Luke 8:26–39).

8. **Gethsemane**—A garden across the Kidron Valley
   from Jerusalem, on the Mount of Olives. Jesus
   brought His disciples to Gethsemane where
   He prayed, asking the Father to take the cup of
   crucifixion from Him. Despite His deep sorrow,
   Jesus accepted His Father's will, while His nearby
   disciples, Peter, James, and John, fell asleep. An armed
   crowd came to Gethsemane, and Jesus was arrested,
   following Judas's betrayal of Him with a kiss. The
   disciples fled as their Master was led away to face the
   Sanhedrin (Matthew 26:36–57).

9. **Jerusalem**—Jesus first visited Jerusalem as an infant,
   when His parents traveled to the city for the Passover,
   then visited again when He was 12 years old. In
   Jerusalem, Satan tempted Jesus to throw Himself down
   from the temple. Early in His ministry, He visited
   Jerusalem and taught at the Temple. But because the
   religious and civil leaders rejected His message and
   even sought to kill Him, Jesus did not spend large
   amounts of time in the city. As He headed toward
   Jerusalem just before His death, Jesus recognized
   that His death had to take place in the city. Jesus was
   arrested outside Jerusalem, tried within it, and crucified

and buried just outside the city, at Golgotha.

10. **Mount Hermon or Mount Tabor**—Scholars believe it was on one of these two mountains that Jesus took His disciples Peter, James, and John to witness His transfiguration. When Jesus and the three disciples descended the mountain, Jesus performed another miracle: healing a demon-possessed son of a man who pleaded with Him for His help after the disciples failed to heal the boy. Jesus used this event to teach His followers the importance of prayer and fasting (Mark 9:1–29).

11. **Nain**—A Galilean city. As Jesus and a crowd of followers came to the city gate, a funeral procession for a young man came out. Jesus had compassion on his mother, a widow, and brought her son back to life (Luke 7:11–15).

12. **Nazareth**—In this village of Galilee, the virgin Mary heard the news that she would bear the Messiah. Here Jesus announced the beginning of His ministry and the fulfillment of the promise of the Good News and liberty for God's people. Furious, the people of his hometown tried to kill Him (Luke 4:28–29). Matthew's account tells us that their unbelief caused Him not to do many miracles there (Matthew 13:58).

13. **Samaria**—During the New Testament era, Samaria was the central Roman province of western Palestine. On the border between Samaria and Galilee, Jesus healed the ten leprous men, only one of whom gave thanks. At Sychar, a place where Jacob dug a well, Jesus discussed spiritual matters with a Samaritan woman,

talked to her about living water, and told her He was
the Messiah she was looking for (John 4:4–26).

14. **The Temple in Jerusalem**—Shortly after His birth,
Jesus was brought to the temple so His parents could
offer a sacrifice. Here Simeon and the prophetess
Anna recognized God's salvation in Jesus. After
their return to Nazareth, Joseph and Mary went to
Jerusalem each year, at Passover. When Jesus was
twelve, they found Him in the temple, talking with
the teachers of the law. Early in His ministry, He went
to the temple and cleared it of the cattle, sheep, and
doves that were sold for sacrifice, declaring, "How
dare you turn my Father's house into a market!" (John
2:16 NIV).

15. **Tyre and Sidon**—People from the area of Sidon
followed Jesus when they heard of the things He had
done. When Jesus received little response from people
in the cities of Israel where He had done many of His
miracles, He cried out that Tyre and Sidon would
have humbly repented, had they seen these things.
Jesus visited the area of Tyre and Sidon, and the Syro-
Phoenician woman called on Him to cast a devil from
her daughter. Because of her persistence, Jesus healed
the girl (Matthew 15:21–29).

15 IMPORTANT WOMEN IN JESUS' LIFE AND MINISTRY

1. **Anna**—A widowed prophetess who lived in the temple and recognized Jesus as the Messiah when He was first brought to the temple as an infant (Luke 2:36).

2. **Joanna**—A woman who followed Jesus and provided for His financial needs. Joanna was the wife of one of King Herod's officials and was later one of the first to learn of and tell others about Jesus' resurrection (Luke 8:3, 24:10).

3. **Mary (His mother)**—Jesus' mother, who as a virgin received the news from an angel that she would bear the Messiah (Luke 1:27–38). Mary traveled to Bethlehem with her betrothed, Joseph. Jesus was born there (Luke 2:1–18), and there Mary saw the shepherds and kings (Matthew 2:1–11) worship Him. Mary stood by the cross and saw her son crucified (John 19:25) and was in the upper room, praying with the disciples after His ascension (Acts 1:14).

4. **Mary of Bethany**—Sister of Lazarus and Martha, Mary of Bethany listened at Jesus' feet while her sister became encumbered in household matters (Luke 10:39–42). When their brother became ill, Martha and Mary called for Jesus. While He delayed, Lazarus died (John 11:28–32). Mary saw her brother Lazarus resurrected by Jesus. She anointed Him with spikenard before His death (John 12:3).

5. **Martha of Bethany**—Sister of Lazarus and Mary.

Jesus became friendly with the family when Martha invited Him to her home in Bethany. Martha, encumbered with serving, asked Jesus to tell Mary to help her, but Jesus pointed out that Mary had chosen the better part—listening to His teaching. When their brother became ill, Martha and Mary called for Jesus. While He delayed, Lazarus died. When Jesus reached Bethany, Martha commented, "If thou hadst been here, my brother had not died" (John 11:21). Jesus pointed out that He was the resurrection and brought her brother back to life.

6. **Mary Magdalene**—Jesus cast seven devils out of her (Mark 16:9). Mary was present throughout the crucifixion of Jesus. Following His resurrection, she came to the tomb with the other women to anoint His body and saw the angels who reported Jesus was raised from the dead. She and the other women told the disciples (Luke 24:9–10). As Mary wept at the tomb, Jesus appeared to her. She did not recognize Him until He spoke her name (John 20:1–18).

7. **Mary, Mother of James and Joses**—She was with Mary Magdalene and other women at the crucifixion of Jesus and at the tomb following His resurrection (Matthew 27:56; Luke 24:10).

8. **Peter's Mother-in-Law**—She was sick with a fever, but Jesus healed her so quickly and completely that she was up serving Him and His followers (Mark 1:29–31).

9. **Salome**—A follower of Jesus who witnessed His death on the cross and later brought spices to anoint His body—only to find it gone due to His resurrection (Mark 15:40, 16:1).

10. **Susanna**—A woman who followed Jesus and provided for His financial needs (Luke 8:3).

11. **Samaritan Woman at the Well**—Jesus spoke with this woman at a well about living water and declared Himself as the Messiah (John 4:4–26). She went back to the city and told the men that she had seen the Messiah, and they came to see Him.

12. **Syrophoenician Woman**—When Jesus traveled to Tyre and Sidon, this unnamed woman insisted that He help her daughter, who had an unclean spirit. Jesus pointed out that He was sent to Israel and compared the woman to a dog. Instead of taking offense, she reminded Him that crumbs fell from the master's table to the dogs. Commending her great faith, Jesus healed her daughter (Matthew 15:22–28).

13. **Woman with the Blood Issue**—This unnamed woman approached Jesus, hoping just to touch His garment so that she could be healed. Jesus recognized her faith and told her she had been made well (Matthew 9:20–22).

14. **A "Daughter of Abraham" with a Spirit of Infirmity**—Jesus healed this woman, who had been infirmed for 18 years, calling her a "daughter of Abraham" (Luke 13:11–16). She immediately walked upright and began praising God.

15. **A Widow in Nain**—Jesus had compassion on this grieving woman and told her to "weep not" over the death of her only son. Jesus then raised the man from the dead (Luke 7:11–15).

25 IMPORTANT SAYINGS OF JESUS

1. **"Ask, and it shall be given you**; seek, and ye shall find; knock, and it shall be opened unto you. For every one that asketh receiveth; and he that seeketh findeth; and to him that knocketh it shall be opened" (Luke 11:9–10).

2. "Behold, **I stand at the door, and knock:** if any man hear my voice, and open the door, I will come in to him, and will sup with him, and he with me" (Revelation 3:20).

3. **"If any man desire to be first,** the same shall be last of all, and servant of all" (Mark 9:35).

4. "Verily I say unto you, Whosoever shall not **receive the kingdom of God as a little child,** he shall not enter therein" (Mark 10:15).

5. **"Judge not, that ye be not judged.** For with what judgment ye judge, ye shall be judged: and with what measure ye mete, it shall be measured to you again" (Matthew 7:1–2).

6. **"I am the bread of life:** he that cometh to me shall never hunger; and he that believeth on me shall never thirst" (John 6:35).

7. "Whosoever drinketh of the water that I shall give him shall never thirst; but the water that I shall give him shall be in him a **well of water springing up into everlasting life"** (John 4:14).

8. "Verily, verily, I say unto thee, **Except a man be born again, he cannot see the kingdom of God"** (John 3:3).

9. **"For God so loved the world,** that he gave his only begotten Son, that whosoever believeth in him should not perish, but have everlasting life" (John 3:16).

10. "After this manner therefore pray ye: **Our Father which art in heaven, hallowed be thy name.** Thy kingdom come, thy will be done in earth, as it is in heaven. Give us this day our daily bread. And forgive us our debts, as we forgive our debtors. And lead us not into temptation, but deliver us from evil: For thine is the kingdom, and the power, and the glory, for ever. Amen" (Matthew 6:9–13).

11. "All power is given unto me in heaven and in earth. **Go ye therefore, and teach all nations,** baptizing them in the name of the Father, and of the Son, and of the Holy Ghost: Teaching them to observe all things whatsoever I have commanded you" (Matthew 28:18–20).

12. **"Lay not up for yourselves treasures upon earth,** where moth and rust doth corrupt, and where thieves break through and steal: But lay up for yourselves treasures in heaven, where neither moth nor rust doth corrupt, and where thieves do not break through nor steal: For where your treasure is, there will your heart be also" (Matthew 6:19–21).

13. "Therefore all things **whatsoever ye would that men should do to you, do ye even so to them:** for this is the law and the prophets" (Matthew 7:12).

14. **"No man can serve two masters:** for either he will hate the one, and love the other; or else he will hold to the one, and despise the other. Ye cannot serve God

and mammon" (Matthew 6:24).

15. "Take heed, and beware of covetousness: for **a man's life consisteth not in the abundance of the things** which he possesseth" (Luke 12:15).

16. "I say unto you, that likewise **joy shall be in heaven over one sinner that repenteth,** more than over ninety and nine just persons, which need no repentance" (Luke 15:7).

17. "Come unto me, all ye that labour and are heavy laden, and I will give you rest. Take my yoke upon you, and learn of me; for I am meek and lowly in heart: and ye shall find rest unto your souls. For **my yoke is easy, and my burden is light**" (Matthew 11:28–30).

18. "Whosoever will come after me, let him deny himself, and take up his cross, and follow me. For whosoever will save his life shall lose it; but **whosoever shall lose his life for my sake and the gospel's, the same shall save it**" (Mark 8:34–35).

19. "Ye have heard that it hath been said, Thou shalt love thy neighbour, and hate thine enemy. But I say unto you, **Love your enemies,** bless them that curse you, do good to them that hate you, and pray for them which despitefully use you, and persecute you" (Matthew 5:43–44).

20. "**A new commandment I give unto you, That ye love one another;** as I have loved you, that ye also love one another. By this shall all men know that ye are my disciples, if ye have love one to another" (John 13:34–35).

21. "The first of all the commandments is, Hear, O Israel; The Lord our God is one Lord: And thou shalt love the Lord thy God with all thy heart, and with all thy soul, and with all thy mind, and with all thy strength: this is the first commandment. And the second is like, namely this, Thou shalt love thy neighbour as thyself. **There is none other commandment greater than these**" (Mark 12:29–31).

22. "If ye have faith as a grain of mustard seed, ye shall say unto this mountain, Remove hence to yonder place; and it shall remove; and **nothing shall be impossible unto you**" (Matthew 17:20).

23. "**If ye forgive men their trespasses, your heavenly Father will also forgive you:** But if ye forgive not men their trespasses, neither will your Father forgive your trespasses" (Matthew 6:14–15).

24. "I **am the way, the truth, and the life:** no man cometh unto the Father, but by me" (John 14:6).

25. "**Seek ye first the kingdom of God,** and his righteousness; and all these things shall be added unto you" (Matthew 6:33).

THE BEATITUDES (DECLARATIONS OF BLESSING)

- Blessed are **the poor in spirit:** for theirs is the kingdom of heaven (Matthew 5:3).

- Blessed are **they that mourn:** for they shall be comforted (Matthew 5:4).

- Blessed are **the meek:** for they shall inherit the earth (Matthew 5:5).

- Blessed are **they which do hunger and thirst after righteousness:** for they shall be filled (Matthew 5:6).

- Blessed are **the merciful:** for they shall obtain mercy (Matthew 5:7).

- Blessed are **the pure in heart:** for they shall see God (Matthew 5:8).

- Blessed are **the peacemakers:** for they shall be called the children of God (Matthew 5:9).

- Blessed are **they which are persecuted for righteousness' sake:** for theirs is the kingdom of heaven (Matthew 5:10).

25 "I AM" STATEMENTS OF JESUS CHRIST

1. I am **The Messiah** (John 4:26).
2. I am **the bread of life** (John 6:35).
3. I am **the living bread** (John 6:51).
4. I am **from [God]** (John 7:29).
5. I am **the light of the world** (John 8:12, 9:5).
6. I am **one that bear witness** of myself (John 8:18).
7. I am **from above** (John 8:23).
8. I am **not of this world.**(John 8:23).
9. **Before Abraham was,** I am (John 8:58).
10. I am **the door of the sheep** (John 10:7).

11. I am **the good shepherd** (John 10:11, 14).

12. I am **the Son of God** (John 10:36).

13. I am **the resurrection, and the life** (John 11:25).

14. I am come **a light into the world** (John 12:46).

15. I am **the way, the truth, and the life** (John 14:6).

16. I am **in the Father,** and the Father in me (John 14:10, 11).

17. I am **in my Father,** and ye in me, and I in you (John 14:20).

18. I am **the true vine** (John 15:1).

19. I am **the vine,** ye are the branches (John 15:5).

20. I am **not of the world** (John 17:14).

21. I am **Alpha and Omega,** the beginning and the ending (Revelation 1:8).

22. I am Alpha and Omega, **the first and the last** (Revelation 1:11).

23. I am **he that liveth, and was dead** (Revelation 1:18).

24. I am **he which searcheth the reins and hearts** (Revelation 2:23).

25. I am **the root and the offspring of David,** and the bright and morning star (Revelation 22:16).

35 "MY FATHER" STATEMENTS OF JESUS

1. "Not every one that saith unto me, Lord, Lord, shall enter into the kingdom of heaven; but he that doeth the will of my Father which is in heaven" (Matthew 7:21).

2. "Whosoever therefore shall confess me before men, him will I confess also before my Father which is in heaven. But whosoever shall deny me before men, him will I also deny before my Father which is in heaven" (Matthew 10:32–33).

3. "All things are delivered unto me of my Father: and no man knoweth the Son, but the Father; neither knoweth any man the Father, save the Son, and he to whomsoever the Son will reveal him" (Matthew 11:27).

4. "For whosoever shall do the will of my Father which is in heaven, the same is my brother, and sister, and mother" (Matthew 12:50).

5. "Blessed art thou, Simon Barjona: for flesh and blood hath not revealed it unto thee, but my Father which is in heaven" (Matthew 16:17).

6. "Take heed that ye despise not one of these little ones; for I say unto you, that in heaven their angels do always behold the face of my Father which is in heaven" (Matthew 18:10).

7. "Again I say unto you, that if two of you shall agree on earth as touching any thing that they shall ask, it shall be done for them of my Father which is in heaven" (Matthew 18:19).

8. "Ye shall drink indeed of my cup, and be baptized with the baptism that I am baptized with: but to sit on my right hand, and on my left, is not mine to give, but it shall be given to them for whom it is prepared of my Father" (Matthew 20:23).

9. "But I say unto you, I will not drink henceforth of this

fruit of the vine, until that day when I drink it new with you in my Father's kingdom" (Matthew 26:29).

10. "O my Father, if it be possible, let this cup pass from me: nevertheless not as I will, but as thou wilt" (Matthew 26:39).

11. "Thinkest thou that I cannot now pray to my Father, and he shall presently give me more than twelve legions of angels?" (Matthew 26:53).

12. "And, behold, I send the promise of my Father upon you: but tarry ye in the city of Jerusalem, until ye be endued with power from on high" (Luke 24:49).

13. "I am come in my Father's name, and ye receive me not: if another shall come in his own name, him ye will receive" (John 5:43).

14. "Verily, verily, I say unto you, Moses gave you not that bread from heaven; but my Father giveth you the true bread from heaven" (John 6:32).

15. "Therefore said I unto you, that no man can come unto me, except it were given unto him of my Father" (John 6:65).

16. "Ye neither know me, nor my Father: if ye had known me, ye should have known my Father also" (John 8:19).

17. "When ye have lifted up the Son of man, then shall ye know that I am he, and that I do nothing of myself; but as my Father hath taught me, I speak these things" (John 8:28).

18. "If I honour myself, my honour is nothing: it is my Father that honoureth me; of whom ye say, that he is your God" (John 8:54).

19. "Therefore doth my Father love me, because I lay down my life, that I might take it again" (John 10:17).

20. "The works that I do in my Father's name, they bear witness of me" (John 10:25).

21. "My Father, which gave them me, is greater than all; and no man is able to pluck them out of my Father's hand" (John 10:29).

22. "I and my Father are one" (John 10:30).

23. "If I do not the works of my Father, believe me not" (John 10:37).

24. "In my Father's house are many mansions: if it were not so, I would have told you. I go to prepare a place for you" (John 14:2).

25. "If ye had known me, ye should have known my Father also: and from henceforth ye know him, and have seen him" (John 14:7).

26. "He that believeth on me, the works that I do shall he do also; and greater works than these shall he do; because I go unto my Father" (John 14:12).

27. "He that hath my commandments, and keepeth them, he it is that loveth me: and he that loveth me shall be loved of my Father, and I will love him, and will manifest myself to him" (John 14:21).

28. "If a man love me, he will keep my words: and my Father will love him, and we will come unto him, and make our abode with him" (John 14:23).

29. "Ye have heard how I said unto you, I go away, and come again unto you. If ye loved me, ye would

rejoice, because I said, I go unto the Father: for my Father is greater than I" (John 14:28).

30. "I am the true vine, and my Father is the husbandman" (John 15:1).

31. "Herein is my Father glorified, that ye bear much fruit; so shall ye be my disciples (John 15:8).

32. "If ye keep my commandments, ye shall abide in my love; even as I have kept my Father's commandments, and abide in his love" (John 15:10).

33. "Henceforth I call you not servants; for the servant knoweth not what his lord doeth: but I have called you friends; for all things that I have heard of my Father I have made known unto you" (John 15:15).

34. "And when he [the Holy Spirit] is come, he will reprove the world of. . .righteousness, because I go to my Father, and ye see me no more" (John 16:8, 10).

35. "Peace be unto you: as my Father hath sent me, even so send I you" (John 20:21).

30 PARABLES OF JESUS

1. The Barren Fig Tree (Luke 13:6–9)
2. The Friend at Midnight (Luke 11:5–8)
3. The Fig Tree (Luke 21:29–31)
4. The Great Banquet (Luke 14:15–24)
5. The Good Samaritan (Luke 10:29–37)
6. The Growing Seed (Mark 4:26–29)

7. The Hidden Treasure (Matthew 13:44)

8. The Laborers in the Vineyard (Matthew 20:1–16)

9. The Lost Coin (Luke 15:8–10)

10. The Lost Sheep (Matthew 18:10–14)

11. The Mustard Seed (Matthew 13:31–32)

12. The Net (Matthew 13:47–50)

13. The Pearl of Great Price (Matthew 13:45–46)

14. The Persistent Widow (Luke 18:1–8)

15. The Pharisee and the Tax Collector (Luke 18:9–14)

16. The Prodigal Son (Luke 15:11–32)

17. The Rich Fool (Luke 12:16–21)

18. The Rich Man and Lazarus (Luke 16:19–31)

19. The Shrewd Manager (Luke 16:1–13)

20. The Sower (Matthew 13:1–9)

21. The Talents (Matthew 25:14–30)

22. The Wicked Tenants (Matthew 21:33–45)

23. The Ten Pounds (Luke 19:11–27)

24. The Ten Virgins (Matthew 25:1–13)

25. The Unmerciful Servant (Matthew 18:25–35)

26. The Unworthy Servant (Luke 17:7–10)

27. The Wedding Feast (Matthew 22:1–14)

28. The Weeds among the Wheat (Matthew 13:24–30)

29. The Wise Servant (Luke 12:35–40)

30. Yeast (Matthew 13:33)

JESUS' SEVEN STATEMENTS FROM THE CROSS

- **Pleading on behalf of His tormenters:** "Father, forgive them; for they know not what they do" (Luke 23:34).

- **Praying to God the Father:** "Eli, Eli, lama sabachthani?" which means "My God, my God, why hast thou forsaken me?" (Matthew 27:46).

- **Speaking to the penitent thief on the cross:** "Verily I say unto thee, Today shalt thou be with me in paradise" (Luke 23:43).

- **Speaking to His mother, Mary:** "Woman, behold thy son!" Speaking to the disciple He loved: "Behold thy mother!" (John 19:26–27).

- "I thirst" (John 19:28).

- "Father, into thy hands I commend my spirit" (Luke 23:46).

- "It is finished!" (John 19:30).

JESUS' POST-RESURRECTION APPEARANCES

- To Mary Magdalene outside the empty tomb (Mark 16:9–11)

- To the other women (Matthew 28:9–10)

- To two disciples on the road to Emmaus (Luke 24:13–32)

- To the eleven remaining apostles (Luke 24:36)

- To Peter (Luke 24:34; 1 Corinthians 15:5)
- To the apostles except for Thomas (John 20:19–25)
- To Thomas (John 20:26–31)
- To seven apostles at the Sea of Galilee (John 21:1–23)
- To five hundred brothers (1 Corinthians 15:6)
- To the eleven apostles in Galilee (Matthew 28:16–20)
- To James (1 Corinthians 15:7)
- At the time of His ascension (Luke 24:36–50)
- To Paul at his conversion (Acts 9:1–19; 1 Corinthians 15:8)

7 | WHAT—OR WHO—IS BEHIND THE NAMES? IMPORTANT BIBLICAL NAMES AND TITLES

50 MOST IMPORTANT NAMES/ TITLES OF GOD

1. Abba, Father (Mark 14:36)
2. Almighty God (Genesis 17:1)
3. Ancient of Days (Daniel 7:9)
4. Consuming Fire (Hebrews 12:28–29)
5. Creator (Isaiah 40:28)
6. Crown of Glory/Diadem of Beauty (Isaiah 28:5)
7. Deliverer (Psalm 70:5)
8. Dwelling Place (Psalm 90:1)
9. Everlasting God (Genesis 21:33)
10. Father (Isaiah 64:8)
11. Father of Our Lord Jesus Christ (Colossians 1:3)
12. Fortress (Jeremiah 16:19)
13. Fountain of Living Waters (Jeremiah 2:13)
14. God of Abraham, Isaac, and Jacob (Exodus 3:15)
15. God of All Comfort (2 Corinthians 1:3)
16. God of Heaven (Nehemiah 1:4)

17. God of My Salvation (Habakkuk 3:17–18)

18. God of Peace (Hebrews 13:20–21)

19. God of the Whole Earth (Isaiah 54:5)

20. Hiding Place (Psalm 32:7)

21. Holy One (Isaiah 43:15)

22. Horn of My Salvation (Psalm 18:2)

23. I Am That I Am (Exodus 3:14)

24. Jah (Psalm 68:4)

25. Jehovah (Exodus 6:3)

26. Jehovahjireh, or the Lord will Provide (Genesis 22:14)

27. Jehovahnissi, or the Lord is our Banner (Exodus 17:15)

28. Jehovahshalom, or the Lord is Peace (Judges 6:23–24)

29. Judge (Psalm 75:7)

30. Judge of All the Earth (Genesis 18:25)

31. King (1 Samuel 12:12)

32. King Eternal, Immortal, Invisible (1 Timothy 1:17)

33. King of Glory (Psalm 24:7–10)

34. Lawgiver (Isaiah 33:22)

35. Light (Psalm 27:1)

36. Living God (Daniel 6:20)

37. Lord of Hosts (Zechariah 8:22)

38. Lord Our Righteousness (Jeremiah 23:6)

39. Lord Who Heals (Exodus 15:26)

40. Majesty on High (Hebrews 1:3)
41. Most High God (Genesis 14:18–19)
42. Potter (Isaiah 64:8)
43. Redeemer (Isaiah 54:8)
44. Refuge (Deuteronomy 33:27)
45. Rock (1 Samuel 2:2)
46. Saviour (Isaiah 45:21)
47. Shepherd (Psalm 23:1)
48. Shield (Psalm 5:12)
49. Strength (Exodus 15:2)
50. Strong Tower (Proverbs 18:10)

16 "OF ISRAEL" NAMES FOR GOD

1. Consolation of Israel (Luke 2:25)
2. Creator of Israel (Isaiah 43:15)
3. Glory of Israel (Luke 2:32)
4. God of Israel (Matthew 15:31)
5. Holy One of Israel (Psalm 78:41)
6. Hope of Israel (Jeremiah 14:7–8)
7. Judge of Israel (Micah 5:1)
8. Light of Israel (Isaiah 10:17)
9. LORD God of Israel (1 Kings 8:23)
10. Mighty One of Israel (Isaiah 1:24)

11. Redeemer of Israel (Isaiah 49:7)

12. Rock of Israel (2 Samuel 23:3)

13. Sceptre out of Israel (Numbers 24:17)

14. Shepherd of Israel (Psalm 80:1)

15. Stone of Israel (Genesis 49:24)

16. Strength of Israel (1 Samuel 15:29)

25 HEBREW NAMES FOR GOD AND THEIR ENGLISH EQUIVALENTS

1. **Adonai**—Lord, Master (Exodus 15:7)

2. **El Channun**—The Gracious God (Jonah 4:2)

3. **El Echad**—The One God (Malachi 2:10)

4. **El Elyon**—The Most High God (Genesis 14:20)

5. **El Emet**—The God of Truth (Psalm 31:5)

6. **El Gibbor**—Mighty God (Isaiah 9:6)

7. **El Hakkadosh**—The Holy God (Isaiah 5:16)

8. **El Hanne'eman**—The Faithful God (Deuteronomy 7:9)

9. **El Olam**—God Everlasting (Genesis 21:33)

10. **El Rachum**—Merciful God (Deuteronomy 4:31)

11. **El Sali**—God My Rock (Psalm 42:9)

12. **El Shaddai**—God Almighty (Genesis 17:1)

13. **El Yeshuati**—God of Our Salvation (Isaiah 12:2)

14. **Immanuel**—God with Us (Isaiah 7:14)

15. **Jehovah Elohim**—God (Genesis 1:1)

16. **Jehovah Melek**—The God Who Is King (Isaiah 33:22)

17. **Jehovah Mekoddishkem**—The Lord Who Sanctifies You (Exodus 31:13)

18. **Jehovah Qanna**—Jealous (Exodus 20:5)

19. **Jehovah Raah**—The Lord My Shepherd (Psalm 23:1)

20. **Jehovah Rapha**—The Lord That Heals (Exodus 15:25–26)

21. **Jehovah Sabbaoth**—The Lord of Hosts (1 Samuel 1:3)

22. **Jehovah Shalom**—The Lord Is Peace (Judges 6:22–24)

23. **Jehovah Shammah**—The Lord Is There (Ezekiel 48:35)

24. **Jehovah Tsidkenu**—The Lord Our Righteousness (Jeremiah 23:6)

25. **Yahweh (YHWH)**—Lord, The Eternal (Exodus 6:3)

25 IMPORTANT TITLES OF JESUS

1. Advocate (1 John 2:1)

2. Alpha and Omega (Revelation 1:8)

3. Author and Finisher of Our Faith (Hebrews 12:2)

4. Bread of Life (John 6:35)

5. Chief Shepherd (1 Peter 5:4)

6. The Christ (1 John 2:22)

7. Faithful and True Witness (Revelation 3:14)

8. God (John 1:1; Hebrews 1:8; Romans 9:5)

9. Great High Priest (Hebrews 4:14)

10. Horn of Salvation (Luke 1:69)

11. I Am (John 8:58)

12. King of Kings, and Lord of Lords (Revelation 19:16)

13. Lamb of God (John 1:29)

14. Last Adam (1 Corinthians 15:45)

15. Light of the World (John 8:12)

16. Lion of the Tribe of Judah (Revelation 5:5)

17. Mediator (1 Timothy 2:5)

18. Messiah (Daniel 9:25–26)

19. Mighty God (Isaiah 9:6)

20. Redeemer (Isaiah 54:5)

21. Resurrection and Life (John 11:25)

22. Saviour (Ephesians 5:23; 2 Peter 2:20)

23. Son of God (John 1:49)

24. Wonderful, Counselor (Isaiah 9:6)

25. The Word (John 1:1)

15 IMPORTANT NAMES/ TITLES OF THE HOLY SPIRIT

1. Comforter (John 14:16)

2. Holy Ghost (John 20:22)

3. Power of the Highest (Luke 1:35)

4. Spirit of Christ (Romans 8:9)
5. The Spirit of Counsel and Might (Isaiah 11:2)
6. Spirit of the Father (Matthew 10:20)
7. Spirit of Glory (1 Peter 4:14)
8. The Spirit of God (Genesis 1:2)
9. Spirit of Grace (Hebrews 10:29)
10. Spirit of Holiness (Romans 1:4)
11. Spirit of Judgment (Isaiah 4:4)
12. Spirit of Life (Romans 8:2)
13. Spirit of Wisdom and Revelation (Ephesians 1:17)
14. Spirit of the Son of God (Galatians 4:6)
15. Spirit of Truth (John 14:17)

10 BIBLICAL NAMES/TITLES FOR THE WRITTEN WORD OF GOD

1. Word of God (Luke 11:28)
2. Word of Life (Philippians 2:16)
3. Word of Christ (Colossians 3:16)
4. The Book (Psalm 40:7)
5. Book of the Law (Deuteronomy 31:26)
6. Holy Scriptures (Romans 1:2)
7. Lively Oracles (Acts 7:38)
8. Scriptures (John 5:39)

9. Sword of the Spirit (Ephesians 6:17)

10. Good Word of God (Hebrews 6:5)

25 NAMES/TITLES FOR THE CHURCH (BELIEVERS AS A GROUP)

1. Assembly of the Saints (Psalm 89:7)

2. Assembly of the Upright (Psalm 111:1)

3. Body of Christ (Ephesians 1:22–23)

4. Bride of Christ (Revelation 21:9)

5. Church of God (Acts 20:28)

6. Church of the Living God (1 Timothy 3:15)

7. Church of the Firstborn (Hebrews 12:23)

8. City of the Living God (Hebrews 12:22)

9. Congregation of Saints (Psalm 149:1)

10. Family in Heaven and Earth (Ephesians 3:15)

11. Flock of God (1 Peter 5:2)

12. General Assembly of the Firstborn (Hebrews 12:23)

13. God's Husbandry and Building (1 Corinthians 3:9)

14. God's Heritage (1 Peter 5:3)

15. Habitation of God (Ephesians 2:22)

16. Heavenly Jerusalem (Hebrews 12:22)

17. House of Christ (Hebrews 3:6)

18. Household of God (Ephesians 2:19)

19. Lamb's Wife (Revelation 21:9)

20. New Jerusalem (Revelation 21:2)

21. Pillar and Ground of the Truth (1 Timothy 3:15)

22. Sheepfold (John 10:1)

23. Spiritual House (1 Peter 2:5)

24. Temple of the Living God (2 Corinthians 6:16)

25. Vineyard (Matthew 21:41)

25 NAMES/TITLES FOR INDIVIDUAL FOLLOWERS OF CHRIST

1. Believers (Acts 5:14)

2. Beloved of God (Romans 1:7)

3. Blessed of the Father (Matthew 25:34)

4. Brethren of Christ (John 20:17)

5. Called of Jesus Christ (Romans 1:6)

6. Children of the Father (Matthew 5:45)

7. Children of the Resurrection (Luke 20:36)

8. Christians (Acts 11:26)

9. Disciples (John 8:31)

10. Friends of God (James 2:23)

11. Friends of Christ (John 15:15)

12. Heirs of God (Galatians 4:7)

13. Holy priesthood (1 Peter 2:5)

14. Joint-heirs with Christ (Romans 8:17)

15. Lambs (John 21:15)

16. Lights of the world (Matthew 5:14)

17. Royal priesthood (1 Peter 2:9)

18. Salt of the earth (Matthew 5:13)

19. Servants of Christ (1 Corinthians 7:22)

20. Sons of God (1 John 3:1–2)

25 TITLES FOR MINISTERS

1. Ambassadors for Christ (2 Corinthians 5:20)

2. Apostles of Jesus Christ (Titus 1:1)

3. Bishops (Philippians 1:1)

4. Deacons (1 Timothy 3:8)

5. Elders (1 Timothy 5:17)

6. Evangelists (2 Timothy 4:5)

7. Fishers of Men (Mark 1:17)

8. Laborers (Matthew 9:38)

9. Messengers of the Church (2 Corinthians 8:23)

10. Ministers of Christ (Romans 15:16)

11. Ministers of the Church (Colossians 1:24–25)

12. Ministers of God (2 Corinthians 6:4)

13. Ministers of the Gospel (Ephesians 3:7)

14. Ministers of the Word (Luke 1:2)

15. Overseers (Acts 20:28)

16. Pastors (Ephesians 4:11)

17. Preachers (Romans 10:14)

18. Servants of the Lord (2 Timothy 2:24)

19. Servants of the Church (2 Corinthians 4:5)

20. Shepherds (Jeremiah 23:4)

21. Soldiers of Christ (Philippians 2:25)

22. Stewards of God (Titus 1:7)

23. Teachers (Ephesians 4:11)

24. Witnesses (Acts 1:8)

25. Workers Together with God (2 Corinthians 6:1)

20 NAMES/TITLES FOR THE DEVIL

1. Abaddon/Apollyon (Revelation 9:11)

2. Accuser of Our Brethren (Revelation 12:10)

3. Adversary (1 Peter 5:8)

4. Beelzebub (Matthew 12:24)

5. Belial (2 Corinthians 6:15)

6. Dragon (Revelation 20:2)

7. The Enemy (Matthew 13:39)

8. Father of Lies (John 8:44)

9. God of This World (2 Corinthians 4:4)

10. Great Red Dragon (Revelation 12:3)

11. Liar (John 8:44)

12. Murderer (John 8:44)

13. Old Serpent (Revelation 12:9)

14. Prince of This World (John 14:30)

15. Prince of the Devils (Matthew 12:24)

16. Prince of the Power of the Air (Ephesians 2:2)

17. Satan (Job 1:6)

18. Serpent (2 Corinthians 11:3)

19. Tempter (Matthew 4:3)

20. Wicked One (Matthew 13:19)

25 NAMES/TITLES FOR THE WICKED/SINNERS

1. Abominable Branches (Isaiah 14:19)

2. Children of Belial (Deuteronomy 13:13)

3. Children of Disobedience (Ephesians 2:2)

4. Children of Hell (Matthew 23:15)

5. Children of the Bondwoman (Galatians 4:31)

6. Children of the Devil (1 John 3:10)

7. Children of the Wicked One (Matthew 13:38)

8. Children of this World (Luke 16:8)

9. Children of Wrath (Ephesians 2:3)

10. Cursed Children (2 Peter 2:14)

11. Enemies of the Cross (Philippians 3:18)
12. Enemies of Righteousness (Acts 13:10)
13. Evildoers (Psalm 37:9)
14. Evil Men (Proverbs 4:14)
15. Fools (Psalm 53:1)
16. Goats (Matthew 25:32)
17. Rebellious Children (Isaiah 30:1)
18. Rebellious Nation (Ezekiel 2:3)
19. Rebellious People (Isaiah 30:9)
20. Reprobates (2 Corinthians 13:5)
21. Transgressors (Psalm 37:38)
22. Vessels of Wrath (Romans 9:22)
23. Wandering Stars (Jude 13)
24. Whited Sepulchres (Matthew 23:27)
25. Ravening Wolves (Matthew 7:15)

35 MOST COMMON MEN'S NAMES

1. Azariah (28 men)
2. Zechariah (27)
3. Shemaiah (25)
4. Maaseiah (21)
5. Meshullam (21)
6. Shimei (18)
7. Hananiah (14)
8. Hashabiah (14)
9. Joel (14)
10. Jonathan (14)
11. Shallum (14)
12. Jehiel (13)

13. Obadiah (13)
14. Benaiah (12)
15. Zichri (12)
16. Eliezer (11)
17. Johanan (11)
18. Joseph (11)
19. Bani (10)
20. Eliel (10)
21. Michael (10)
22. Nathan (10)
23. Nethaneel (10)
24. Adaiah (9)
25. Amariah (9)
26. Elam (9)
27. Hanan (9)
28. Jeshua (9)
29. Mattaniah (9)
30. Seraiah (9)
31. Shelemiah (9)
32. Shephatiah (9)
33. Simon (9)
34. Zadok (9)
35. Zebadiah (9)

18 MOST COMMON WOMEN'S NAMES

1. Mary (7 women)
2. Maachah (6)
3. Tamar (3)
4. Abigail (2)
5. Abihail (2)
6. Adah (2)
7. Ahinoam (2)
8. Azubah (2)
9. Bashemath (2)
10. Deborah (2)
11. Mahalath (2)
12. Milcah (2)
13. Miriam (2)
14. Naamah (2)
15. Sarah (2)
16. Shelomith (2)
17. Shua (2)
18. Timna (2)

19 UNISEX NAMES IN SCRIPTURE

1. Abiah (2 men, 1 woman)
2. Abihail (3 men, 2 women)
3. Abijah (5 men, 1 woman)
4. Ahlai (1 man, 1 woman)
5. Aholibamah (1 man, 1 woman)
6. Anah (2 men, 1 woman)
7. Athaliah (2 men, 1 woman)
8. Ephah (2 men, 1 woman)
9. Gomer (1 man, 1 woman)
10. Hushim (2 men, 1 woman)
11. Joanna (1 man, 1 woman)
12. Maacah (1 men, 1 woman)
13. Maachah (4 men, 6 women)
14. Michaiah (4 men, 1 woman)
15. Noadiah (1 man, 1 woman)
16. Noah (1 man, 1 woman)
17. Puah (2 men, 1 woman)
18. Shelomith (5 men, 2 women)
19. Timna (1 man, 2 women)

BIBLICAL PEOPLE WHOSE NAMES WERE CHANGED

- **Abram to Abraham (Genesis 17:5)**—When Abram was ninety years old, God made a covenant with him and changed his name to Abraham. The name Abram means "high father," while the name Abraham means "father of a multitude."

- **Sarai to Sarah (Genesis 17:15)**—God gave Sarai, wife of Abram (Abraham), the name Sarah after He promised she would bear a child, even though she was ninety years old. The name Sarai means "controlling" and the name Sarah means "noble."

- **Jacob to Israel (Genesis 32:28, 35:10)**—God renamed Jacob Israel when Jacob wrestled with God at Peniel. After renaming him, God again appeared to Jacob, confirmed His covenant promises, and blessed him. The name Jacob means "supplanter," and the name Israel means "he will rule as God."

- **Simon to Peter (Cephas) (John 1:42)**—Jesus gave Simon Bar-Jona the new name Cephas (or Peter), which means "rock," after Andrew, Peter's brother, brought him to meet Jesus for the first time.

- **Saul of Tarsus to Paul (Acts 13:9)**—In Luke's narrative in the book of Acts, he begins referring to Saul by his Latin name, Paul in Acts 13:9. The Latin name Paul means "little," while the Hebrew name Saul means "asked."

- **Daniel to Belteshazzar (Daniel 1:6–7)**—The Hebrew prophet Daniel received the Babylonian name Belteshazzar when he entered King Nebuchadnezzar's service.

- **Hananiah to Shadrach (Daniel 1:6–7)**—Hananiah, one of Daniel's friends, received the Babylonian name Shadrach at the same time Daniel received the name Belteshazzar. The name Hananiah means "God has favored."

- **Mishael to Meshach (Daniel 1:6–7)**—A friend and companion of the prophet Daniel who received the Babylonian name Meshach. The Hebrew name Mishael means "who is what God is?"

- **Azariah to Abed-nego (Daniel 1:6–7)**—The third of Daniel's companions in exile. His Hebrew name was exchanged for the Babylonian name Abed-nego. The Hebrew name Azariah means "God has helped."

THINGS TO FOCUS ON: IMPORTANT CONCEPTS, VERSES, AND PASSAGES IN THE BIBLE

WHAT EACH BOOK IS ABOUT

- **Genesis**—God creates the world and chooses a special people.

- **Exodus**—God delivers His people, the Israelites, from slavery in Egypt.

- **Leviticus**—A holy God explains how to worship Him.

- **Numbers**—Faithless Israelites wander forty years in the wilderness of Sinai.

- **Deuteronomy**—Moses reminds the Israelites of their history and God's laws.

- **Joshua**—The Israelites capture and settle the Promised Land of Canaan.

- **Judges**—Israel goes through cycles of sin, suffering, and salvation.

- **Ruth**—Loyal daughter-in-law depicts God's faithfulness, love, and care.

- **1 Samuel**—Israel's twelve tribes unite under a king.

- **2 Samuel**—David becomes Israel's greatest king—but with major flaws.

- **1 Kings**—Israel divides into rival northern and southern nations.

- **2 Kings**—Both Jewish nations are destroyed for their disobedience to God.

- **1 Chronicles**—King David's reign is detailed and analyzed.

- **2 Chronicles**—The history of Israel, from Solomon, through division, to destruction.

- **Ezra**—Spiritual renewal begins after the Jews return from exile.

- **Nehemiah**—Returning Jewish exiles rebuild the broken walls of Jerusalem.

- **Esther**—Beautiful Jewish girl becomes queen, saves fellow Jews from slaughter.

- **Job**—God allows human suffering for His own purposes.

- **Psalms**—Ancient Jewish songbook showcases prayers, praise—and complaints—to God.

- **Proverbs**—Pithy, memorable sayings encourage people to pursue wisdom.

- **Ecclesiastes**—Apart from God, life is empty and unsatisfying.

- **Song of Solomon**—Married love is a beautiful thing worth celebrating.

- **Isaiah**—A coming Messiah will save people from their sins.

- **Jeremiah**—After years of sinful behavior, Judah will be punished.

- **Lamentations**—A despairing poem over the destruction of Jerusalem.

- **Ezekiel**—Though Israel is in exile, the nation will be restored.

- **Daniel**—Faithful to God in a challenging setting, Daniel is blessed.

- **Hosea**—Prophet's marriage to prostitute reflects God's relationship with Israel.

- **Joel**—Locust plague pictures God's judgment on His sinful people.

- **Amos**—Real religion isn't just ritual, but treating people with justice.

- **Obadiah**—Edom will suffer for participating in Jerusalem's destruction.

- **Jonah**—Reluctant prophet, running from God, is swallowed by giant fish.

- **Micah**—Israel and Judah will suffer for their idolatry and injustice.

- **Nahum**—Powerful, wicked Nineveh will fall before God's judgment.

- **Habakkuk**—Trust God even when He seems unresponsive or unfair.

- **Zephaniah**—A coming "day of the Lord" promises heavy judgment.

- **Haggai**—Jews returning from exile need to rebuild God's temple.

- **Zechariah**—Jewish exiles should rebuild their temple—and anticipate their Messiah.

- **Malachi**—The Jews have become careless in their attitude toward God.

- **Matthew**—Jesus fulfills the Old Testament prophecies of a coming Messiah.
- **Mark**—Jesus is God's Son, a suffering servant of all people.
- **Luke**—Jesus is savior of all people, whether Jew or Gentile.
- **John**—Jesus is God Himself, the only Saviour of the world.
- **Acts**—The Holy Spirit's arrival heralds the beginning of the Christian church.
- **Romans**—Sinners are saved only by faith in Jesus Christ.
- **1 Corinthians**—An apostle tackles sin problems in the church at Corinth.
- **2 Corinthians**—Paul defends his ministry to the troubled Corinthian church.
- **Galatians**—Christians are free from restrictive Jewish laws.
- **Ephesians**—Christians are all members of Jesus' "body," the church.
- **Philippians**— "Friendship letter" between the apostle Paul and a beloved church.
- **Colossians**—Jesus Christ is supreme—over everyone and everything.
- **1 Thessalonians**—Jesus will return to gather His followers to Him.

- **2 Thessalonians**—Christians should work until Jesus returns.

- **1 Timothy**—Pastors are taught how to conduct their lives and churches.

- **2 Timothy**—The apostle Paul's final words to a beloved coworker.

- **Titus**—Church leaders are instructed on their lives and teaching.

- **Philemon**—Paul begs mercy for a runaway slave converted to Christianity.

- **Hebrews**—Jesus is better than any Old Testament person or sacrifice.

- **James**—Real Christian faith is shown by one's good works.

- **1 Peter**—Suffering for the sake of Jesus is noble and good.

- **2 Peter**—Beware of false teachers within the church.

- **1 John**—Jesus was real man, just as He is real God.

- **2 John**—Beware false teachers, who deny Jesus' physical life on earth.

- **3 John**—Church leaders must be humble, not proud.
- **Jude**—Beware of heretical teachers and their dangerous doctrines.

- **Revelation**—God will judge evil and reward His saints.

25 IMPORTANT BIBLICAL CONCEPTS

1. God is our Creator, but He is also our loving heavenly Father.

2. God is our Provider who meets our physical and spiritual needs.

3. God wants His people to worship and love Him.

4. God blesses obedience and punishes disobedience.

5. God is a God of mercy, love, and grace.

6. God sometimes allows suffering for His own purposes and for our good.

7. God has identified Himself in three persons—the Father, the Son, and the Holy Spirit.

8. God is completely holy, and He requires that His people be holy too.

9. God wants His people to find satisfaction and fulfillment in Him.

10. We are blessed when we remain faithful to God, especially in a challenging setting.

11. Real religion isn't just ritual; it's loving God and other people in our words and actions.

12. Faith—believing God and the promises in His Word—is at the heart of our relationship with God; without faith, we cannot please God.

13. We are to take God and our relationship with Him very seriously, not carelessly.

14. Jesus fulfills all the Old Testament prophecies of a coming Messiah.

15. Jesus is God's Son, the suffering servant of all people.

16. Jesus is saviour of all people of all races and nationalities.

17. Jesus is God Himself, the only Saviour of the world.

18. Sinners are saved only by faith in Jesus Christ.

19. Jesus will one day return to gather His followers to Him.

20. Though we aren't saved by our works, real Christian faith is demonstrated in good works.

21. Suffering for Jesus is noble and good.

22. God disciplines those He loves.

23. Jesus was real man, just as He is real God.

24. God rewards humility but resists pride.

25. God will one day judge evil and reward His saints.

25 GREAT PROMISES OF SCRIPTURE

1. **Abundant Life in Christ**—"I am come that they might have life, and that they might have it more abundantly" (John 10:10; also see John 14:19; Romans 6:8, 11; Ephesians 2:1, 5–6; 1 John 5:12).

2. **Adoption into God's Family through Christ**—"As many as are led by the Spirit of God, they are the sons of God. For ye have not received the spirit of bondage again to fear; but ye have received the Spirit of adoption, whereby we cry, Abba, Father" (Romans

8:14–15; also see Romans 9:26; 2 Corinthians 6:18; Galatians 4:4–7; 1 John 3:1–2).

3. **Christ Prays for Us**—"Wherefore he is able also to save them to the uttermost that come unto God by him, seeing he ever liveth to make intercession for them" (Hebrews 7:25; also see Romans 8:34).

4. **Christ's Return**—"The Lord himself shall descend from heaven with a shout, with the voice of the archangel, and with the trump of God: and the dead in Christ shall rise first: then we which are alive and remain shall be caught up together with them in the clouds, to meet the Lord in the air: and so shall we ever be with the Lord" (1 Thessalonians 4:16–17; also see Matthew 24:30; Mark 14:62; John 14:3; 1 Corinthians 4:5; 2 Timothy 4:8; Revelation 1:7).

5. **Confident Access to God**—"Having therefore, brethren, boldness to enter into the holiest by the blood of Jesus, by a new and living way, which he hath consecrated for us, through the veil, that is to say, his flesh" (Hebrews 10:19–20; also see Ephesians 2:18, 3:12; 1 John 5:14–16).

6. **God Provides Deliverance in Times of Trouble**—"Many are the afflictions of the righteous: but the LORD delivereth him out of them all" (Psalm 34:19; also see Job 8:20–21; Psalm 18:27–28; 42:11, 71:20).

7. **Eternal Life with God in Heaven**—"In my Father's house are many mansions: if it were not so, I would have told you. I go to prepare a place for you. And if I go and prepare a place for you, I will come again,

and receive you unto myself; that where I am, there ye may be also" (John 14:2–3; also see Romans 2:7; 1 Corinthians 2:9; Hebrews 4:9; 1 Peter 9; 2 Peter 3:13; Revelation 3:4).

8. **Forgiveness of Sin**—"If we confess our sins, he is faithful and just to forgive us our sins, and to cleanse us from all unrighteousness" (1 John 1:9; also see Psalm 65:3, 103:9–12; Isaiah 43:25, 44:22; Micah 7:18–19; Matthew 26:28; Ephesians 1:7; Hebrews 10:17; Revelation 1:5).

9. **God Hears Our Prayers**—"Ask, and it shall be given you; seek, and ye shall find; knock, and it shall be opened unto you: for every one that asketh receiveth; and he that seeketh findeth; and to him that knocketh it shall be opened" (Matthew 7:7–8; also see Psalm 4:3, 50:15; Proverbs 15:29; Matthew 21:22; James 5:15–16).

10. **God's Enduring Love**—"I have loved thee with an everlasting love: therefore with lovingkindness have I drawn thee" (Jeremiah 31:3; also Zephaniah 3:17; John 16:27; Ephesians 2:4; 2 Thessalonians 2:16).

11. **God's Gift of His Spirit**—"If ye then, being evil, know how to give good gifts unto your children: how much more shall your heavenly Father give the Holy Spirit to them that ask him?" (Luke 11:13; also see Proverbs 1:23; Isaiah 32:15; John 14:16–18; Galatians 3:14; 2 Timothy 1:14).

12. **God's Mercy**—"The LORD thy God is a merciful God; he will not forsake thee, neither destroy thee"

(Deuteronomy 4:31; also see Exodus 33:19; Psalm 103:13; Isaiah 30:18, 48:9).

13. **God Will Never Abandon You**—"Zion said, The LORD hath forsaken me, and my Lord hath forgotten me. Can a woman forget her sucking child, that she should not have compassion on the son of her womb? yea, they may forget, yet will I not forget thee. Behold, I have graven thee upon the palms of my hands; thy walls are continually before me" (Isaiah 49:14–16; also see Psalm 9:10, 94:14; Isaiah 54:9–10; Jeremiah 32:40; Hebrews 13:5).

14. **Guidance from Above**—"And the LORD shall guide thee continually" (Isaiah 58:11; also see Deuteronomy 32:10–12; Psalm 23:2–3, 73:24; Isaiah 30:21, 61:8).

15. **Help in Overcoming Temptation**—"God is faithful, who will not suffer you to be tempted above that ye are able; but will with the temptation also make a way to escape, that ye may be able to bear it" (1 Corinthians 10:13; also see Romans 8:37; 2 Corinthians 12:9; Hebrews 2:18; 2 Peter 2:9; 1 John 4:4).

16. **Justification through Jesus Christ**—"Being justified freely by his grace through the redemption that is in Christ Jesus" (Romans 3:24; also see Acts 13:39; 2 Corinthians 5:21).

17. **No Condemnation**—"There is therefore now no condemnation to them which are in Christ Jesus, who walk not after the flesh, but after the Spirit" (Romans 8:1; Also see Romans 8:33–34).

18. **Peace from God**—"Be careful for nothing; but

in every thing by prayer and supplication with thanksgiving let your requests be made known unto God. And the peace of God, which passeth all understanding, shall keep your hearts and minds through Christ Jesus" (Philippians 4:6–7; also see Leviticus 26:6; Psalm 29:11, 119:165; Isaiah 26:12).

19. **Power from God to Persevere**—"And I give unto them eternal life; and they shall never perish, neither shall any man pluck them out of my hand. My Father, which gave them me, is greater than all; and no man is able to pluck them out of my Father's hand" (John 10:28–29; also see Romans 8:38–39; 1 Corinthians 1:8; Philippians 1:6; 1 Thessalonians 5:23– 24; 2 Thessalonians 3:3).

20. **Provision from God**—"But seek ye first the kingdom of God, and his righteousness; and all these things shall be added unto you" (Matthew 6:33; also see Psalm 23:1, 37:3; Matthew 6:26; Philippians 4:19; 1 Timothy 6:6, 17).

21. **Reconciled to God through Christ**—"Much more then, being now justified by his blood, we shall be saved from wrath through him. For if, when we were enemies, we were reconciled to God by the death of his Son, much more, being reconciled, we shall be saved by his life" (Romans 5:9–10; also see 2 Corinthians 5:18–19; Ephesians 2:13–17; Colossians 1:21–23; Hebrews 2:17).

22. **Rewards for Seeking God**—"He that cometh to God must believe that he is, and that he is a rewarder of them that diligently seek him" (Hebrews 11:6; also

see 1 Chronicles 28:9; 2 Chronicles 15:2; Psalm 9:10; Jeremiah 29:13; Amos 5:4; Acts 17:27).

23. **Victory over the Devil**—"I have written unto you, young men, because ye are strong, and the word of God abideth in you, and ye have overcome the wicked one" (1 John 2:14; also see Romans 16:20; James 4:7; 1 John 5:18).

24. **Victory over the World**—"Be of good cheer; I have overcome the world" (John 16:33; also see John 17:15; Galatians 1:4, 6:14; 1 John 5:4–5).

25. **God Keeps All His Promises**—"Know therefore that the LORD thy God, he is God, the faithful God, which keepeth covenant and mercy with them that love him and keep his commandments to a thousand generations" (Deuteronomy 7:9; also see Numbers 23:19; Psalm 89:34; Isaiah 46:11; Romans 4:21; 2 Timothy 2:13; Hebrews 6:18).

66 GREAT VERSES TO MEMORIZE (ONE FROM EACH BIBLE BOOK)

1. "And he [Abram] believed in the LORD; and he counted it to him for righteousness" (Genesis 15:6).

2. "Thou shalt have no other gods before me" (Exodus 20:3).

3. "Ye shall be holy; for I [God] am holy" (Leviticus 11:44).

4. "The LORD is longsuffering, and of great mercy, forgiving iniquity and transgression" (Numbers 14:18).

5. "Thou shalt love the LORD thy God with all thine heart, and with all thy soul, and with all thy might" (Deuteronomy 6:5).

6. "Choose you this day whom ye will serve … as for me and my house, we will serve the LORD" (Joshua 24:15).

7. "And the LORD said unto Gideon, The people that are with thee are too many for me to give the Midianites into their hands, lest Israel vaunt themselves against me, saying, Mine own hand hath saved me" (Judges 7:2).

8. "Whither thou goest, I will go; and where thou lodgest, I will lodge: thy people shall be my people, and thy God my God" (Ruth 1:16).

9. "Behold, to obey is better than sacrifice, and to hearken than the fat of rams" (1 Samuel 15:22).

10. "Who am I, O Lord GOD? and what is my house, that thou hast brought me hitherto?" (2 Samuel 7:18).

11. "Hear me, O LORD, hear me, that this people may know that thou art the LORD God, and that thou hast turned their heart back again" (1 Kings 18:37).

12. "And it came to pass, when they were gone over, that Elijah said unto Elisha, Ask what I shall do for thee, before I be taken away from thee. And Elisha said, I pray thee, let a double portion of thy spirit be upon me" (2 Kings 2:9).

13. "I will settle him in mine house and in my kingdom for ever: and his throne shall be established for evermore" (1 Chronicles 17:14).

14. "LORD God of Israel, there is no God like thee in the

heaven, nor in the earth; which keepest covenant, and shewest mercy unto thy servants, that walk before thee with all their hearts" (2 Chronicles 6:14).

15. "Ezra had prepared his heart to seek the law of the LORD, and to do it, and to teach in Israel statutes and judgments" (Ezra 7:10).

16. "Think upon me, my God, for good, according to all that I have done for this people" (Nehemiah 5:19).

17. "Esther obtained favor in the sight of all them that looked upon her" (Esther 2:15).

18. "Naked came I out of my mother's womb, and naked shall I return thither: the LORD gave, and the LORD hath taken away; blessed be the name of the LORD" (Job 1:21).

19. "I will lift up mine eyes unto the hills, from whence cometh my help. My help cometh from the LORD" (Psalm 121:1–2).

20. "Trust in the LORD with all thine heart; and lean not unto thine own understanding" (Proverbs 3:5).

21. "Remember now thy Creator in the days of thy youth" (Ecclesiastes 12:1).

22. "He brought me to the banqueting house, and his banner over me was love" (Song of Songs 2:4).

23. "All we like sheep have gone astray; we have turned every one to his own way; and the LORD hath laid on him the iniquity of us all" (Isaiah 53:6).

24. "Behold, as the clay is in the potter's hand, so are ye in mine hand, O house of Israel" (Jeremiah 18:6).

25. "It is of the LORD's mercies that we are not consumed, because his compassions fail not" (Lamentations 3:22).

26. "I have no pleasure in the death of him that dieth, saith the Lord GOD: wherefore turn yourselves, and live ye" (Ezekiel 18:32).

27. "We do not present our supplications before thee for our righteousnesses, but for thy great mercies" (Daniel 9:18).

28. "I [God] drew them [Israel] with cords of a man, with bands of love" (Hosea 11:4).

29. "Whosoever shall call on the name of the LORD shall be delivered" (Joel 2:32).

30. "Prepare to meet thy God, O Israel" (Amos 4:12).

31. "Upon Mount Zion shall be deliverance" (Obadiah 17).

32. "I will pay that that I have vowed. Salvation is of the LORD" (Jonah 2:9).

33. "He hath shewed thee, O man, what is good; and what doth the LORD require of thee, but to do justly, and to love mercy, and to walk humbly with thy God?" (Micah 6:8).

34. "The LORD is good, a strong hold in the day of trouble; and he knoweth them that trust in him" (Nahum 1:7).

35. "The just shall live by his faith" (Habakkuk 2:4).

36. "The LORD thy God in the midst of thee is mighty; he will save, he will rejoice over thee with joy" (Zephaniah 3:17).

37. "Be strong, all ye people of the land, saith the LORD, and work: for I am with you, saith the LORD of hosts" (Haggai 2:4).

38. "Turn ye unto me, saith the LORD of hosts, and I will turn unto you" (Zechariah 1:3).

39. "Return unto me, and I will return unto you" (Malachi 3:7).

40. "Ask, and it shall be given you; seek, and ye shall find; knock, and it shall be opened unto you" (Matthew 7:7).

41. "Come ye after me, and I will make you to become fishers of men" (Mark 1:17).

42. "For where your treasure is, there will your heart be also" (Luke 12:34).

43. "For God so loved the world, that he gave his only begotten Son, that whosoever believeth in him should not perish, but have everlasting life" (John 3:16).

44. "Neither is there salvation in any other: for there is none other name under heaven given among men, whereby we must be saved" (Acts 4:12).

45. "And we know that all things work together for good to them that love God, to them who are the called according to his purpose" (Romans 8:28).

46. "Though I speak with the tongues of men and of angels, and have not charity, I am become as sounding brass, or a tinkling cymbal" (1 Corinthians 13:1).

47. "For he hath made him to be sin for us, who knew no sin; that we might be made the righteousness of God in him" (2 Corinthians 5:21).

48. "The fruit of the Spirit is love, joy, peace, longsuffering, gentleness, goodness, faith, meekness, temperance: against such there is no law" (Galatians 5:22–23).

49. "By grace are ye saved through faith; and that not of yourselves: it is the gift of God: not of works, lest any man should boast" (Ephesians 2:8–9).

50. "Be careful for nothing; but in every thing by prayer and supplication with thanksgiving let your requests be made known unto God" (Philippians 4:6).

51. "Set your affection on things above, not on things on the earth" (Colossians 3:2).

52. "For the Lord himself shall descend from heaven with a shout, with the voice of the archangel, and with the trump of God: and the dead in Christ shall rise first" (1 Thessalonians 4:16).

53. "Brethren, be not weary in well doing" (2 Thessalonians 3:13).

54. "Christ Jesus came into the world to save sinners; of whom I am chief" (1 Timothy 1:15).

55. "Thou therefore endure hardness, as a good soldier of Jesus Christ" (2 Timothy 2:3).

56. "Not by works of righteousness which we have done, but according to his mercy he saved us, by the washing of regeneration, and renewing of the Holy Ghost" (Titus 3:5).

57. "I thank my God, making mention of thee always in my prayers, hearing of thy love and faith, which thou

hast toward the Lord Jesus, and toward all saints"
(Philemon 1:4–5).

58. "Wherefore seeing we also are compassed about with
so great a cloud of witnesses, let us lay aside every
weight, and the sin which doth so easily beset us,
and let us run with patience the race that is set before
us, looking unto Jesus the author and finisher of our
faith" (Hebrews 12:1–2).

59. "The effectual fervent prayer of a righteous man
availeth much" (James 5:16).

60. "Be sober, be vigilant; because your adversary the
devil, as a roaring lion, walketh about, seeking whom
he may devour" (1 Peter 5:8).

61. "The Lord is not slack concerning his promise, as
some men count slackness; but is longsuffering to us-
ward, not willing that any should perish, but that all
should come to repentance" (2 Peter 3:9).

62. "Beloved, let us love one another: for love is of
God.... God is love" (1 John 4:7–8).

63. "This is love, that we walk after his commandments"
(2 John 1:6).

64. "I have no greater joy than to hear that my children
walk in truth" (3 John 1:4).

65. "Ye should earnestly contend for the faith which was
once delivered unto the saints" (Jude 1:3).

66. "Worthy is the Lamb that was slain to receive power,
and riches, and wisdom, and strength, and honour,
and glory, and blessing" (Revelation 5:12).

21 GREAT BIBLE PASSAGES FOR STUDY

1. **Genesis 1–3**—Creation and the Entrance of Sin

2. **Genesis 6:9–8:22**—The Flood

3. **Exodus 20:3–17**—The Ten Commandments

4. **Joshua 1**—God's Instructions to Joshua

5. **1 Samuel 17:12–54**—David's Battle with Goliath

6. **1 Kings 8:12–54**—Solomon's Prayer

7. **Psalm 1**—A Blessed Man

8. **Psalm 23**—The Shepherdhood of God

9. **Isaiah 6:1–8**—Isaiah's Call

10. **Daniel 6**—Daniel in the Lions' Den

11. **Luke 2:1–20**—Christ's Birth

12. **Matthew 3:13–4:11**—Jesus' Baptism and Temptation

13. **Matthew 5–7**—Christ's Sermon on the Mount

14. **Matthew 22:34–40**—Two Great Commandments

15. **Matthew 27:27–28:10**—Christ's Death and Resurrection

16. **Luke 11:2–4**—A Model Prayer

17. **John 3:1–21**—The New Birth in Christ

18. **John 4:1–42**—The Samaritan Woman at the Well

19. **Acts 2**—Believers Receive the Holy Spirit; the Church Built

20. **1 Corinthians 13**—The Love Chapter

21. **Hebrews 11**—The "Faith Hall of Fame"